GENETICS

THE SCIENCE OF LIFE

Heredity

SUSAN SCHAFER

Sharpe Focus

an imprint of M.E. Sharpe, Inc.

Sharpe Focus
An imprint of M.E. Sharpe, Inc.
80 Business Park Drive
Armonk, NY 10504
www.sharpe-focus.com

Library of Congress Cataloging-in-Publication Data

Schafer, Susan.
  Heredity / [Susan Schafer].
      p. cm. -- (Genetics: the science of life)
  Includes bibliographical references and index.
  ISBN 978-0-7656-8136-2 (hardcover : alk. paper)
  1. Heredity--Juvenile literature. 2. Genetics--Juvenile literature. I.
Title.
  QH437.5.S34 2009
  576.5--dc22

                          2008008105

Editor: Peter Mavrikis
Production Manager: Henrietta Toth
Editorial Assistant and Photo Research: Alison Morretta
Program Coordinator: Cathy Prisco
Design: Patrice Sheridan
Line Art: FoxBytes

Printed in Malaysia

9 8 7 6 5 4 3 2 1

PICTURE CREDITS: Cover: ScienceFoto/Getty Images; pages 4, 18, 20 (right), 45, 50, 74 (right), 77:
Stone/Getty Images; pages 6, 7 (top), 7 (bottom), 8, 11, 13, 16, 24, 28, 29, 35, 40, 41, 52, 67: FoxBytes; pages
9 (top), 12, 30, 62, 68 (right): Science Faction/Getty Images; pages 9 (middle), 9 (bottom), 10, 20 (left), 21,
58, 68 (left), 78, 83: Visuals Unlimited/Getty Images; pages 14, 72: ScienceFoto/Getty Images; page 32: GAP
Photos/Getty Images; pages 34, 79: Hulton Archive/Getty Images; pages 39, 74 (left): Getty Images; page 44:
Discovery Channel Images/Getty Images; pages 46, 48: AFP/Getty Images; pages 54, 55: Dorling
Kindersley/Getty Images; page 56: Altrendo/Getty Images; pages 57, 70: Taxi/Getty Images; page 61: Hola
Images/Getty Images; page 64: © iStockphoto.com; pages 81, 84: 3D4Medical.com/Getty Images; page 82:
Time & Life Pictures/Getty Images; back cover: Photographer's Choice/Getty Images.

Contents

Bean cells dividing by mitosis. Each cell forms two cells.

CHAPTER 1

Passing It On

Have you ever passed a note to someone in class? Inside the note is a special message from one person to another. Heredity is like that, except the messages are the genes that are passed from parents to offspring. It all begins with a single cell, which is the vehicle for carrying information from generation to generation.

BODIES: ONE CELL, MANY CELLS

When one cell becomes two, all of the information from the original cell ends up in each of the new cells. Many people think that clones are freaks of nature, but cells clone themselves all the time (including when identical twins are formed). When cells reproduce, they make exact copies of all their parts. This form of reproduction is called **asexual reproduction** because it requires only one parent cell. The parent cell is not male or female, although it may come from a male or female body. It is just a cell— a body cell, to be exact.

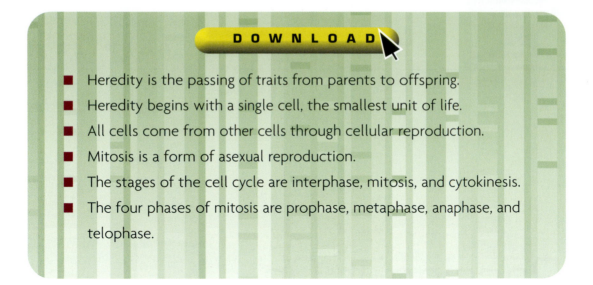

DOWNLOAD

- Heredity is the passing of traits from parents to offspring.
- Heredity begins with a single cell, the smallest unit of life.
- All cells come from other cells through cellular reproduction.
- Mitosis is a form of asexual reproduction.
- The stages of the cell cycle are interphase, mitosis, and cytokinesis.
- The four phases of mitosis are prophase, metaphase, anaphase, and telophase.

A body that is made of only one cell is called **unicellular**. Bacteria, **amoebas,** and most algae are unicellular. If a body is made of two or more cells, it is called **multicellular**. All multicellular plants and animals, including humans, begin life as a unicellular organism at the moment the sperm **fertilizes** the egg. These microsopic, one-celled organisms are called **zygotes,** or fertilized eggs.

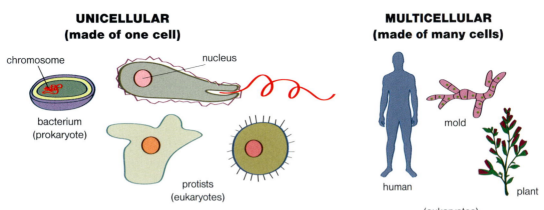

UNICELLULAR
(made of one cell)

chromosome

nucleus

bacterium
(prokaryote)

protists
(eukaryotes)

MULTICELLULAR
(made of many cells)

mold

human

plant

(eukaryotes)

Unicellular organisms are usually so small a microscope is needed to see them. Multicellular organisms can grow larger by adding more cells. The cells may be specialized to perform different jobs, making multicellular organisms more complex.

EMBRYO

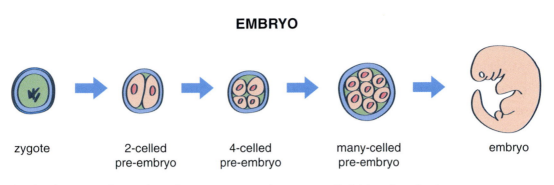

| zygote | 2-celled pre-embryo | 4-celled pre-embryo | many-celled pre-embryo | embryo |

The development of an embryo from a zygote involves many cell divisions by mitosis.

The zygote reproduces asexually and becomes a two-celled organism. From that point forward, the body is multicellular. Every time cells reproduce, the number of cells in the body is doubled. Two cells become four, four become eight, and so on. The result of this multiplication of cells is an **embryo**, a plant or an animal in its first stage of growth.

Stem Cells and Differentiation

The early embryo's cells are all alike. These are known as **stem cells**. Just as the leaves of a tree sprout from a stem, all body cells come from stem cells. Stem cells have the ability to turn into any kind of cell, depending on which genes are "switched on" by special chemicals in the cell. The cells are then **differentiated,** or specialized, and become heart cells, skin cells, stomach cells, nerve cells, and so on. If the genes that control the development of the

DIFFERENTIATED CELLS

stem cell

nerve cells

muscle cells

Stem cells become different kinds of cells (differentiated) depending upon which genes begin working.

heart are activated, stem cells become heart cells. If skin genes are activated, they become skin cells.

Once a cell is differentiated, it loses its ability to change into another kind of cell because unneeded genes are permanently "switched off." Scientists are trying to learn how to turn genes on and off artificially. By switching off genes, they could turn differentiated cells back into stem cells. By switching on genes, they could turn stem cells into any kind of cell they wanted to. They could grow new tissues and organs for people who needed them, repair defective cells, and cure diseases.

As body cells reproduce, the body grows. The greater the number of cells there are, the larger the body is. When cells are damaged or old cells die, other cells reproduce to replace them. The process begins with **DNA** (deoxyribonucleic acid) and involves many **organelles**, which are structures inside a cell that have special jobs.

Organelles

Mitochondria (*my-toe-KAHN-dree-uh; singular* mitochondrion) are organelles that produce the energy needed for all of a cell's activities,

ORGANELLES

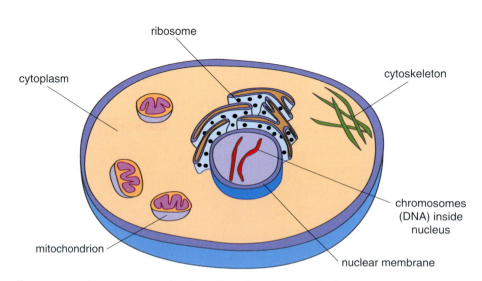

Organelles are special structures inside of a cell, each with a specific function or job.

POP·UP

Bacteria come in many sizes and shapes. Most are so small that a special microscope must be used to see them. A few can be seen with the naked eye. The three basic bacterial shapes are coccus *(KAWK-us)*, bacillus *(buh-SILL-us)*, and spirillum *(spuh-RILL-em)*. Cocci are named for the Greek word for berry because they are round. Bacillus are rod-shaped and get their name from the Latin for small staff. Spirillum, which is Latin for coil, are twisted like springs.

Some bacteria live in your mouth, excreting sticky sugars that help the bacteria stick to your teeth, which is what forms plaque. Others ooze a jelly-like material that wraps them in a protective capsule. The capsule helps them avoid infection-fighting white blood cells in your body.

Staphylococcus aureus bacteria (staph, for short) are shaped like spheres or berries. They live naturally in the nose and on the skin of about one-third of the human population, sometimes causing skin infections such as pimples.

Lactobacillus is a rod-shaped bacterium often used to make cheese, yogurt, pickles, and other fermented foods.

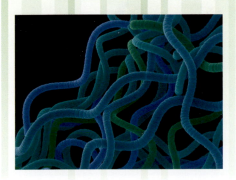

Spirulina bacteria, found in many oceans, are twisted into a spiral shape.

including reproduction. **Ribosomes** make the proteins needed for chemical reactions, such as copying the DNA and breaking down the nucleus. The nucleus must rupture in order for DNA to be released. If this did not occur, the DNA would be trapped in the nucleus and would be unable to get to new cells.

Cytoplasm (*SIGH-tuh-plahz-um*) is a fluid with a consistency somewhat like hair gel that surrounds and cushions the organelles. Tube-like structures crisscross the cytoplasm to form a **cytoskeleton**, or cell skeleton. The cytoskeleton holds the organelles in place and provides the tiny threads needed to transport **chromosomes** during cell reproduction.

THE BACTERIAL SPLIT

Bacteria reproduce asexually by **binary fission** (*BY-nair-ee FIZSH-un*). *Bi-* means two and *fission* means to split. With no nucleus and only one chromosome, a bacterium simply **replicates** or copies the DNA in its chromosomes, moves one copy to each side, and then splits in two. Each half grows into a new adult.

The original cell is called the parent or mother cell. The two cells that are formed are called daughter cells, but they are not female. Scientists needed an easier way to talk about the different cells and felt it was simpler to say "daughter cells" than to say "the two cells that came from the original cell."

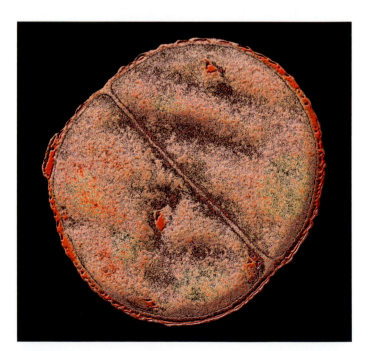

A bacterium splitting in two by binary fission.

BINARY FISSION

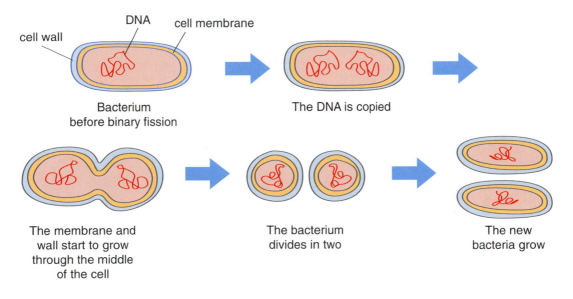

Bacteria reproduce by a type of cell division called binary fission.

In the right environment, a bacterium might divide every twenty minutes or so, which is how diseases spread. For example, if a boy touches a desk that had been touched by someone else who was sick, a single bacterium could be transferred from the desk to a finger. Subsequently, if the boy rubbed his eye, touched his mouth, or picked his nose, that single bacterium could stick to his body **tissues**.

The human mouth, nose, and eyes (which are connected to the nose by the tear ducts) provide a perfect warm, wet environment where bacterium can thrive. In about twenty minutes, that one bacterium would become two, the two would become four, and potentially every twenty minutes the population could double. Someone who is infected with one bacterium at 10 A.M. could have as many as 69 billion bacteria throughout his nose and throat by 10 P.M. As bacteria feed, they **excrete**, or give off, wastes that irritate and kill cells. This causes infected tissues to swell and form mucous. When you get sick, is it any wonder that your nose clogs with green snot and your throat hurts so badly you can hardly swallow?

ALERT !

Thousands of *Escherichia coli,* or *E. coli,* bacteria live in your intestines where they make vitamin K and other products that help you digest fats. They also help fight off disease-causing organisms that you swallow with your food. Without them, you could not live. Sometimes, however, people are infected with a harmful **strain** of *E. coli,* which produces a powerful toxin and causes severe—even life-threatening—diarrhea.

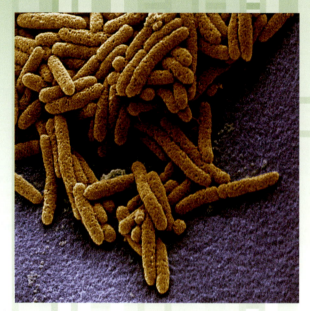

Escherichia coli (or *E. coli*) is a common bacterium that lives naturally in the lower intestine of warm-blooded animals, helping them to digest their food. Some strains, however, can cause severe food poisoning.

PHASE ME

Plant and animal cells reproduce asexually using a process called **mitosis** (*my-TOH-sis*). Technically speaking, mitosis refers to the forming of two new nuclei out of one. Once that happens, the mother cell can divide, separating the two nuclei, one into each new daughter cell. Because each nucleus contains a copy of the original DNA, each daughter cell is

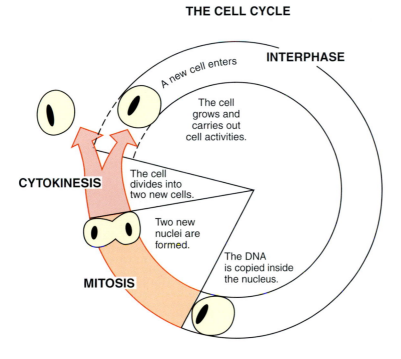

THE CELL CYCLE

INTERPHASE

A new cell enters

The cell grows and carries out cell activities.

CYTOKINESIS

The cell divides into two new cells.

Two new nuclei are formed.

The DNA is copied inside the nucleus.

MITOSIS

Plant and animal cells go through several stages of their life in what is called the cell cycle. Most of the cell's life is spent in interphase, where it grows and carries out cell activities. Near the end of interphase, it copies its DNA to get ready for reproduction. During mitosis, two new nuclei form, one for each new cell formed during cell division, or cytokinesis. Each new cell will enter interphase, and the cycle repeats.

identical to the mother cell. The resulting cells are natural clones: skin cells make more skin cells; nerve cells make more nerve cells.

Mitosis is only one part of cell reproduction. The entire process is called the **cell cycle**, which includes **interphase**, mitosis, and **cytokinesis** (*sigh-toe-keh-NEE-sis*). During interphase, the cell grows and gets ready for mitosis. After mitosis, cytokinesis divides the cell in two. The newly formed cells enter interphase again, and the whole cycle repeats. Over the course of one lifetime, body cells cycle through thousands and thousands of lives.

Depending on the type of cell and the conditions in which it lives, an average cell cycle takes about twenty hours. Most of that time is spent in interphase. Only about an hour is spent in mitosis and cytokinesis. Specific events occur in each stage in a continual process, running smoothly through each stage like a skateboarder rolling from jump to jump or a ballet dancer moving from one position to the next.

During interphase, the cell's **metabolism** (*muh-TAH-boll-ih-zum*) is extremely active, taking in nutrition, producing energy, building organelles, excreting wastes, and growing. The cell replicates, or copies, its DNA so

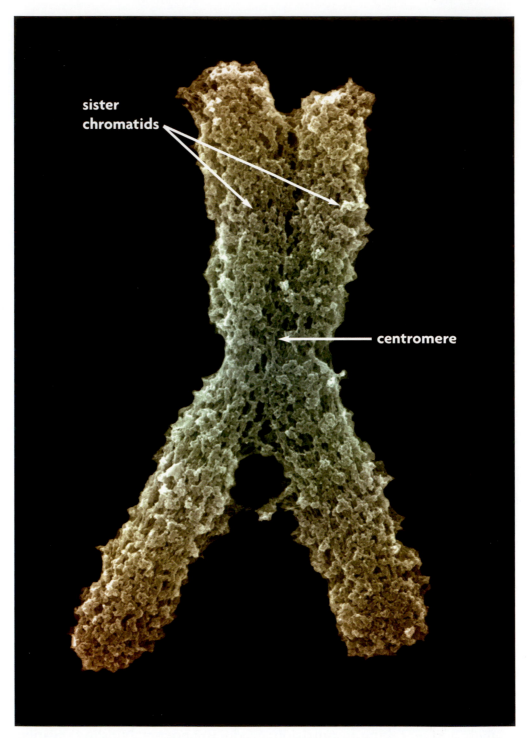

sister chromatids

centromere

One duplicated chromosome (made of coiled and condensed DNA) forms two sister chromatids. The chromatids are attached at the centromere.

that by the end of interphase the nucleus holds two copies of the DNA, one copy for each of the new nuclei that will be formed in mitosis.

When DNA replicates, it unzips down the middle, separating the two long sides of the strand. Then each side rebuilds the side that it is missing, creating two new strands that are identical to the original strand. The new strands, however, do not totally separate. They are held together at a spot called the **centromere**.

The two strands with their centromere form one chromosome. Each side is called a **chromatid**. Together they are called sister chromatids. Again, the two sides are not female. Scientists use the term "sister" to indicate that the two sides are related because they were made from the same DNA.

PMAT

Mitosis includes four phases: prophase, metaphase, anaphase, and telophase. This is easily remembered using the acronym PMAT. When housebreaking a puppy, a mat of newspapers can be placed on the floor. When the puppy has to pee, he is placed on the pee mat . . . PMAT: prophase, metaphase, anaphase, telophase.

The prefix *pro-* means "before," so prophase is the phase that comes before the others. During prophase, the DNA **condenses** or coils into chromosomes, and the membrane around the nucleus breaks down. The DNA must condense so the chromosomes are less likely to get tangled when they are moved around the cells.

When the nuclear membrane breaks down in animal cells, two organelles called **centrioles** (*SEN-tree-ohlz*) move to opposite ends of the cell and form two poles. (Picture a cell as the planet Earth with the North Pole at one end and the South Pole at the other.) The centrioles organize tiny threads called **spindle fibers** that attach to the centromere of the chromosomes, moving them like puppets on strings. Plant cells do not have centrioles, but they are still able to organize spindle fibers during mitosis.

To illustrate what happens during the second stage of mitosis (metaphase), picture two fishermen (centrioles) standing on the opposite shores of a lake. They cast into the lake and each hooks a fish that is an identical twin (sister chromatids). The twin fish, however, are joined in the middle with super glue (centromere). If the fishermen pull on their lines (spindle fibers), the conjoined fish will move.

In metaphase, the spindle fibers pull on the chromosomes until they are lined up in the middle of the cell. A simple way to remember this is to think of metaphase and middle, which both start with the letter *m*.

Once the chromosomes are lined up like ducks on a pond, the cell is ready for anaphase. During anaphase, the centromere breaks and the sister chromatids are pulled to opposite ends of the cell. Imagine the two fishermen pulling so hard on the lines that the twin fish rip apart at the super-glue. One fish would be reeled in to one side of the lake, and the other fish would be reeled to the opposite side of the lake. (Just think anaphase and apart; they both start with the letter *a*.)

Anaphase ensures that a copy of the DNA ends up in each of the new daughter cells. If both chromatids were pulled to the same side of the cell, one cell would have twice the DNA it needed (the original plus the copy) and the other cell would have no DNA. Too much DNA causes disease or cell death; too little causes death because the cell has no instructions. Once the two chromatids pull apart at the centromere, each becomes a chromosome.

The final phase of mitosis is telophase. The prefix *telo* means "end." One complete set of chromosomes sits at each end of the cell. As the

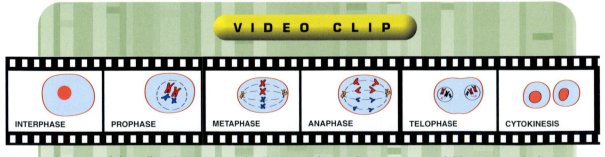

VIDEO CLIP

INTERPHASE   PROPHASE   METAPHASE   ANAPHASE   TELOPHASE   CYTOKINESIS

The steps of the cell cycle in an animal cell: (1) Interphase—the DNA is copied; (2) Mitosis—which includes (2A) Prophase: the chromosomes (DNA) condense and the nuclear membrane breaks down; (2B) Metaphase: the chromosomes line up along the middle of the cell; (2C) Anaphase: the chromatids are pulled apart and are pulled to opposite ends of the cell; and (2D) Telophase: chromosomes unwind and two new nuclei form; (3) Cytokinesis—the cell divides in two.

chromosomes unwind, new nuclear membranes form around them, forming two new nuclei.

Finally, in a burst of movement, cytokinesis divides the cytoplasm in two. *Cyto* means "cell" and *kinesis* means "movement." In animal cells, this division occurs when the cell membrane, which surrounds the cell and protects it from the outside world, pinches off in the middle like a long balloon twisted into two sections. In plant cells, a cell wall surrounds the cell membrane, so a tough plate spreads across the middle of the cell like a knife thrust through an apple, splitting the cell in two.

When the cell finally divides, the daughter cells are only about half the size of the mother cell, so they must reenter interphase in order to grow and build new organelles. Then they will replicate their DNA, and the whole process will begin again. It's a good thing you can't feel mitosis. Just think how many times your cells have been pinched in two just since you started reading this!

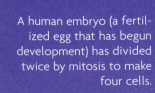

A human embryo (a fertil-
ized egg that has begun
development) has divided
twice by mitosis to make
four cells.

CHAPTER 2

Reinventing the Past

You find an old family album in the attic of your grandparent's house. Inside you discover a photograph of an ancestor who lived nearly 200 years ago. Except you seem to be looking at yourself! Same eyes, same nose, same chin. How could this be? Your resemblance to your relatives is the result of heredity and a process called **meiosis** *(my-OH-sis)*. Meiosis ensures that genes from both sides of a family are passed on to the young. Your genes were passed on to you from your parents, who got them from their parents, who got them from their parents, who got them from their parents . . . well, you get the idea. Therefore, you could have some of the same exact genes that an ancestor carried long ago. Imagine visiting an Egyptian museum and seeing yourself in a portrait painted in the year 500!

IT TAKES TWO

Sex cells, or **gametes** *(GAA-meets)*, are made inside special sex organs in the body through meiosis. Males produce gametes called sperm, and females produce gametes called eggs. Gametes are used for **sexual reproduction,**

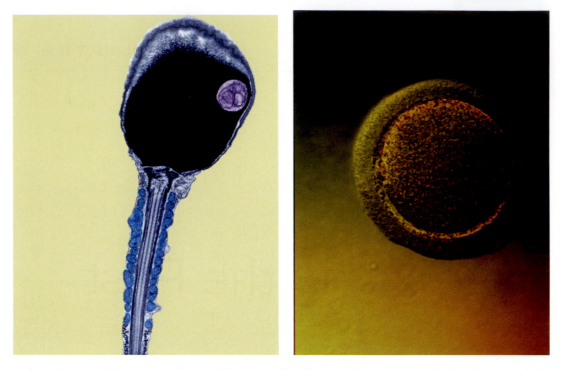

Left: A close up of the head and part of the tail, or flagellum, of a human sperm. The head contains half the normal number of chromosomes, or 23. *Right:* An unfertilized human egg also contains half the normal number of chromosomes, or 23. When a sperm unites with an egg, the chromosome number of the newly created individual returns to 46.

which requires two parents (the male and the female). Each parent contributes half its chromosomes, and therefore half its genes, to each gamete. When the two gametes—sperm and egg—unite, the new individual, called a zygote, has all of the genes it needs to survive.

It is like putting wheels on a bike. The frame of the bike will not work without the wheels. The wheels are useless without the frame; but put them together and they make a whole, functioning machine. The egg cannot survive without the sperm, and vice versa. Together they make a whole, working organism. Most plants and animals, including many single-celled organisms, use meiosis to pass on their genes to their offspring, or young. *Meiosis* means "to make smaller" in Greek.

In meiosis, a cell divides twice to form four cells. The four cells are not identical. Each has the potential to make a unique individual if fertilization takes place. Fertilization is the union of the sperm and egg, which restores

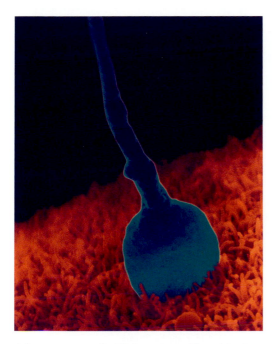

A human sperm fertilizing an egg. The whipping of the tail, or flagellum, forces the head of the sperm through the cell membrane of the egg. The egg then gives off special chemicals that prevent any other sperm from entering.

the original chromosome number of the parents. The original chromosome number is called the **diploid** (*DIP-loyd*) or "double" number. Diploid means that each chromosome exists in pairs. Therefore, diploid cells have two sets of chromosomes: one set that was contributed by the sperm of the male and one set that was contributed by the egg of the female. Each species that reproduces sexually has a characteristic diploid number of chromosomes. For humans it is 46, 23 from the father and 23 from the mother.

In a diploid cell, the two sets of chromosomes are **homologous** to each other. (Homologous comes from the Greek word *homologos*, which means "agreeing.") For every chromosome in

DOWNLOAD

- Meiosis produces sex cells.
- Meiosis is also called reduction division because resulting sex cells contain only half the normal number of chromosomes.
- Male sex cells are called sperm; female sex cells are called eggs.
- Fertilization is the union of a sperm with an egg.
- The eight phases of meiosis, in sequential order, are prophase I, metaphase I, anaphase I, telophase I, prophase II, metaphase II, anaphase II, telophase II.

POP-UP

Comparing Mitosis and Meiosis

Mitosis	**Meiosis**
Asexual reproduction	Sexual reproduction
Occurs in all body cells (except in sex organs)	Occurs only in specialized sex organs
Four phases	Eight phases
Chromosomes do not pair	Chromosomes pair
Genes do not cross over and recombine	Genes cross over and recombine
One cell makes two cells	One cell makes four cells
Daughter cells genetically identical	Daughter cells not genetically identical
Chromosome number stays the same	Chromosome number cut in half
Needed for individual cells to survive	Needed for sexually reproducing species to survive

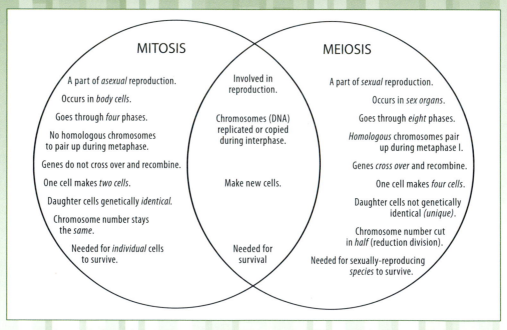

MITOSIS

MEIOSIS

A part of *asexual* reproduction.

Occurs in *body cells*.

Goes through *four* phases.

No homologous chromosomes to pair up during metaphase.

Genes do not cross over and recombine.

One cell makes *two cells*.

Daughter cells genetically *identical*.

Chromosome number stays the *same*.

Needed for *individual* cells to survive.

Involved in reproduction.

Chromosomes (DNA) replicated or copied during interphase.

Make new cells.

Needed for survival

A part of *sexual* reproduction.

Occurs in *sex organs*.

Goes through *eight* phases.

Homologous chromosomes pair up during metaphase I.

Genes *cross over* and recombine.

One cell makes *four cells*.

Daughter cells not genetically identical *(unique)*.

Chromosome number cut in *half* (reduction division).

Needed for sexually-reproducing *species* to survive.

A Venn diagram of the differences and similarities between mitosis and meiosis. The left circle represents how mitosis is different from meiosis. The right circle represents how meiosis is different from mitosis. The area in the middle where the two circles overlap represents how mitosis and meiosis are alike.

one set, there is a matching chromosome in the other set. The genes along both chromosomes will be in the same place, although the actual characteristics carried on the genes might be different.

For example, a particular gene on one chromosome, such as the one that determines the thickness of your eyebrows, would be found in the same place on the other chromosome. However, one chromosome might hold the gene for thick eyebrows and the other might hold the gene for thin eyebrows. To illustrate, it would be like holding two beaded necklaces side by side. They are homologous in that they both have the same type and number of beads, but the beads at any one spot may be different colors.

Sex cells are **haploid**, from the Greek for "simple," because they have only one set of unpaired chromosomes. The haploid number for humans is 23 because there are 23 unpaired chromosomes in the sperm and 23 unpaired chromosomes in the egg. When the two haploid sex cells join during fertilization, they form a diploid cell. Human body cells are diploid because they contain 23 pairs of chromosomes, or a total of 46.

Each living **species** on Earth has a specific number of chromosomes. Some have one; some have more than 200. Species that reproduce asexually by mitosis can have any number of chromosomes. If the parent has one chromosome, the new cells also have one. Species that reproduce sexually must have an even number of chromosomes because the number of chromosomes is cut in half during meiosis. An odd number of chromosomes cannot be divided equally in half when two new cells form. Because the chromosome number is halved, meiosis is also called reduction division.

DOUBLE DIVISION

Once meiosis is complete and the gametes form, they must be fertilized. If a sperm does not fertilize an egg, both sex cells will die. With half the chromosomes, they do not have all of the instructions they need in order to survive.

A diploid cell must replicate, or copy, its DNA to make sister chromatids before it can go through meiosis. After replication, the cell is still diploid because the sister chromatids are attached together by the centromere. They

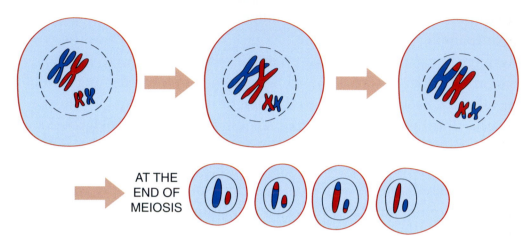

RECOMBINATION (cross over)
DURING PROPHASE I OF MEIOSIS

AT THE
END OF
MEIOSIS

Usually, all of the homologous pairs of chromosomes in a cell cross over and recombine during prophase I of meiosis. This results in the creation of four sex cells, each with a unique set of gene combinations. Recombination increases variety in a species.

will not pull apart and become separate chromosomes until later. One chromosome can have two sister chromatids and still be a single chromosome.

Once the process begins, the cell divides twice. In the first stage, meiosis I, two cells are formed, each with half the original number of chromosomes. Meiosis II results in four gametes.

Remember PMAT, the phases of mitosis? Meiosis uses the same names. Meiosis I includes prophase I, metaphase I, anaphase I, and telophase I. What would be the phases of meiosis II?

Prophase I

Just as in mitosis, the chromosomes in prophase I of meiosis coil tightly and condense, but before the nuclear membrane breaks down, homologous chromosomes or homologues line up alongside each other. The genes on one chromosome (from the sex cell of one parent) move close to the same genes on the homologue (from the sex cell of the other parent). Then they cross over, or trade genes, in a process called **recombination**.

Recombination does not take place between sister chromatids on the same chromosome. Instead, it takes place between nonsister chromatids, which are found on opposite homologous chromosomes. The arms of the nonsister chromatids twist and wind around each other. Chromosomes are either maternal, from the mother, or paternal, from the father. Special chemicals cut out one or more genes from the maternal chromosome and the same genes are cut from the paternal chromosome. The two gene pieces swap places, creating gene patterns that have never existed before. The maternal chromosome now has genes from the father's family line and vice versa.

The other two nonsister chromatids remain unchanged. In the resulting four sex cells, one will contain an unchanged paternal chromosome, one will contain an unchanged maternal chromosome, one will contain a paternal chromosome with a bit of maternal DNA, and one will contain a maternal chromosome with a bit of paternal DNA.

Metaphase I

Once recombination has occurred and spindle fibers are attached to centromeres, the chromosomes move toward the middle plate of the cell. But instead of lining up in a single row as occurs in mitosis, they line up in homologous pairs across the middle or equator of the cell, like couples in a line at a square dance. The way they line up determines the direction they will move during anaphase I.

For example, if the maternal homologue of the first chromosome pair is on one side of the equator of the cell and the maternal homologue of the second chromosome pair is on the opposite side, those maternal chromosomes will go in different directions. The same will happen with each homologous pair for the species, which would be a total of 23 for people.

Chance determines which side the chromosomes line up on and, therefore, the direction they travel. The division of chromosomes varies greatly. There may be one maternal and 22 paternal homologues on one side and one paternal and 22 maternal homologues on the other. Or there may be 5 maternal with 18 paternal on one side and 18 maternal with 5 paternal on the other. In humans, researchers have calculated that with 23 pairs of chromosomes, an individual can produce 8.4 million different gene combinations in their sperm or eggs.

ALERT !

Meiosis ensures that the number of chromosomes in cells does not double with each generation. If the chromosome number were not cut in half, zygotes would have twice the number of chromosomes they should have. For example, if a human sperm with 46 chromosomes fertilized an egg with 46 chromosomes, the zygote would have 92 chromosomes. With every generation, the number would double, which would end in the eventual death of the species.

If our egg and sperm cells were just like our body cells and contained 23 pairs of chromosomes, their fusion during fertilization would create a cell with 46 chromosome pairs, or 92 chromosomes total. To prevent this from happening and to ensure a stable number of chromosomes throughout the generations, a special type of cell division is needed to halve the number of chromosomes in egg and sperm cells. This special process is meiosis.

Anaphase I

Anaphase I is triggered when the fibers that are attached to the centromeres of the chromosomes shorten, which causes the chromosomes to pull apart. The homologous chromosome pairs separate, depending on how they happened to line up during metaphase I. This random separation of homologous chromosomes is called **independent assortment**. At this point, each homologue still has both of its chromatids.

Telophase I

When the homologous pairs separate and arrive at opposite sides of the cell, each side has half the normal number of chromosomes. The condensed chromosomes uncoil, and once cytokinesis pinches the cell in two, the whole process begins again. The second division of meiosis is more like mitosis, except that the cells start out with only half of the original number of chromosomes.

Prophase II and Metaphase II

During prophase II, each chromosome still consists of the two sister chromatids, although they may no longer be exactly alike because of crossover. They coil and condense once again, and new spindle fibers form to attach to the chromosomes and move them toward the middle of the cell for metaphase II, where they line up in a single row.

Anaphase II and Telophase II

During anaphase II, the sister chromatids pull apart and move to opposite poles. In telophase II, the chromosomes uncoil and lengthen, new nuclear membranes form, and the two cells divide into four haploid gametes. Each new cell has a single copy of each chromosome.

When meiosis occurs in males, the cytoplasm of the original cell is equally divided among four sperm. Any of the four could fertilize an egg. However, when females produce eggs, most of the cytoplasm is put into one big cell. The other three cells have little cytoplasm and do not mature. An egg needs to be big. If it is fertilized, it will provide the nourishment needed for the new zygote to grow.

In many species, females do not need to make as many gametes as a male. The eggs they produce stay inside of their bodies where they are protected. But sperm, which look like microscopic tadpoles, have to leave the male's body to find the egg. Many sperm may die along the way and so many more are needed to ensure fertilization of the egg.

Any species with two sexes—male and female—uses meiosis to form sex cells. Recombination and independent assortment ensure that when the sex cells combine to form young, the result is a unique organism rather than a clone of a parent. The process of meiosis is similar to making a collage. Many pieces are put together to create something new.

Meiosis creates variety in a species, which increases the species' chances for survival. If every individual in a population were produced by mitosis, they would all be exactly the same and, therefore, would all be susceptible to the same diseases or environmental changes. For example, if an environment

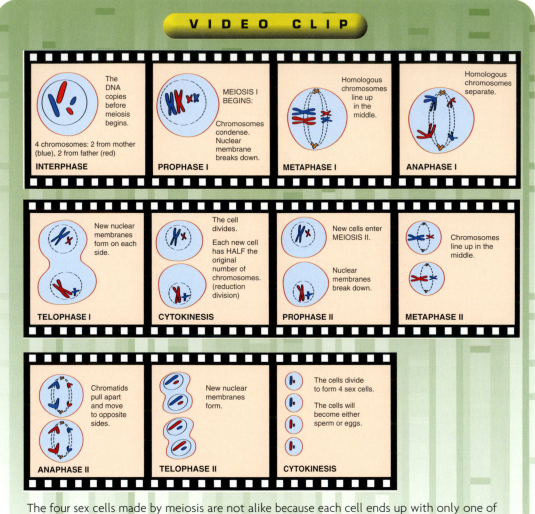

VIDEO CLIP

The four sex cells made by meiosis are not alike because each cell ends up with only one of the homologous pairs of chromosomes. Chance determines which way the chromosomes are pulled during anaphase I. In the example, one long chromosome from the father was pulled to the same side as the short one from the mother, but both chromosomes from the father could have ended up on the same side.

changed from hot to cold and none of the animals living there had a gene for thick fur, the entire population might perish. However, if some individuals had genes for thick fur, they would be more likely to survive. Any thin-furred individuals might still be lost, but the population overall would be saved. Instead of becoming extinct, it would become better **adapted** to its environment.

LIFE CYCLE OF A FLOWERING PLANT

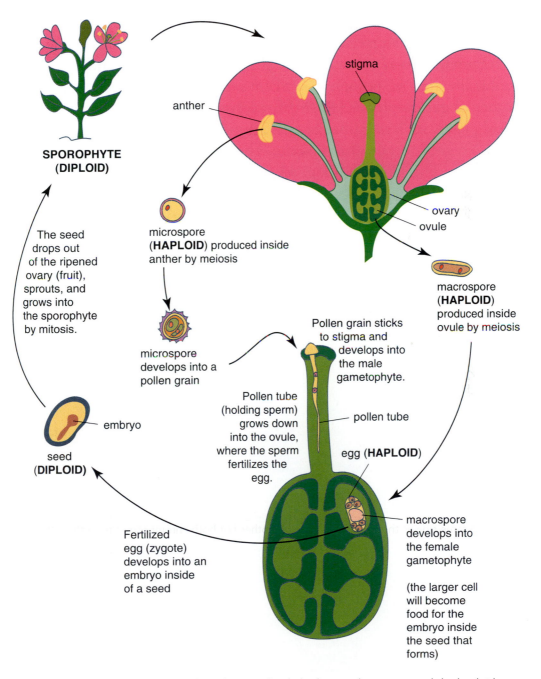

SPOROPHYTE (DIPLOID)

The seed drops out of the ripened ovary (fruit), sprouts, and grows into the sporophyte by mitosis.

anther

stigma

ovary
ovule

microspore (**HAPLOID**) produced inside anther by meiosis

macrospore (**HAPLOID**) produced inside ovule by meiosis

microspore develops into a pollen grain

Pollen grain sticks to stigma and develops into the male gametophyte.

Pollen tube (holding sperm) grows down into the ovule, where the sperm fertilizes the egg.

pollen tube

egg (**HAPLOID**)

embryo

seed (**DIPLOID**)

Fertilized egg (zygote) develops into an embryo inside of a seed

macrospore develops into the female gametophyte

(the larger cell will become food for the embryo inside the seed that forms)

A simplified life cycle of a flowering plant showing the diploid sporophyte stage and the haploid gametophyte stage.

THE DOUBLE LIFE OF PLANTS

Animals that reproduce sexually have the ability to create gametes, which then fuse to make a new animal. But most complex land plants lead a double life: first as **sporophytes** (*SPOR-oh-fyts*), which produce spores, and then as **gametophytes** (*gah-MEE-toh-fyts*), which produce gametes. Typical plants, such as bushes or trees, are sporophytes. They are diploid, with two copies of each chromosome. The sporophyte undergoes meiosis to make spores. The spores are haploid, with half the chromosomes of the sporophyte.

Female spores are called megaspores because they are large, while the

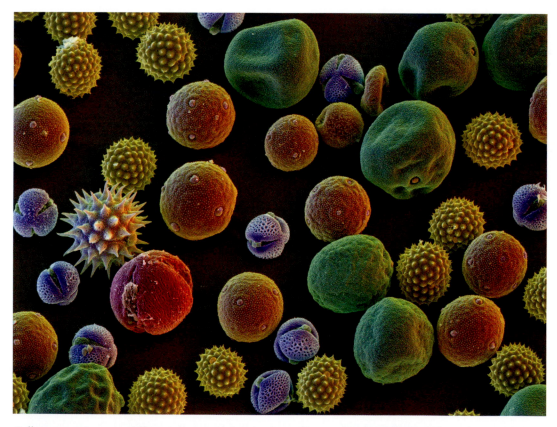

Pollens come in many different shapes and sizes, depending on the plants that produce them. Some, such as those from grasses and ragweed, can cause severe allergies in people.

smaller male spores are called microspores. Instead of joining together to make a new plant, the spores reproduce asexually by mitosis and grow into gametophytes that are still haploid. Male gametophytes then produce sperm; female gametophytes produce eggs. In flowering plants, gameto-phytes are found inside the flower of the sporophyte. The male gameto-phyte grows a thick, spiny wall around it and becomes **pollen**. Sperm forms inside the pollen. Think of that the next time pollen gets in your nose and gives you allergies—you are actually inhaling plant sperm! The female gametophyte grows into an ovule, which will hold the eggs of the female.

Pollination occurs when the pollen from one flower reaches the ovule of another flower, by wind, water, insect, or other means. A tube from the pollen grows into the ovule, allowing the sperm to fertilize the egg. The resulting zygote, which is now diploid again, becomes a seed. The seed undergoes asexual mitosis to grow back into the sporophyte, which is the plant as we know it.

Plant or animal, meiosis ensures that the proper number of genes is passed on to each new generation. To survive and be healthy, offspring need the right number of chromosomes for their particular species. Your body cells live and die inside of you, and meiosis ensures that you will continue to live on in any offspring created by your gametes.

The white flower of the pea plant helped Gregor Mendel discover some of the secrets of heredity.

CHAPTER 3

Mendel and His Peas

Gregor Mendel was the first person to officially study heredity. As a monk in Europe during the mid-1800s, he was responsible for growing food and herbs in the monastery garden. Mendel was particularly interested in garden peas and how their traits or characteristics were passed on from one generation to another. Thanks to Mendel, the field of **genetics**—the scientific study of heredity—was born.

THE HIDDEN SECRETS OF THE PEA

Mendel's experiments provided the evidence to show that certain "units of inheritance," as he called them, were responsible for passing on physical characteristics, or **traits**. He did not call the units *genes*, and the discovery of chromosomes would come later, but Mendel showed that he could predict the characteristics of young based on the characteristics of the parents.

Pea plants normally reproduce by **self-pollination**. This is the transfer of **pollen**, which produces sperm, from one flower to the eggs of the same flower or another flower on the same plant. Mendel observed that the pea

Gregor Mendel studied the inheritance of traits in pea plants, laying the groundwork for later studies of genetics.

plants with white flowers always produced more pea plants with white flowers and his purple-flowering pea plants only produced young with purple flowers. He referred to this as breeding "true." Mendel called his true-breeding plants **purebreds**. A purebred is produced when two parents with the same trait always produce the same trait in their young.

Next, Mendel crossed the purebred purple-flowered plants with purebred white-flowered plants using **cross-pollination**. First, he cut the **anthers** from the white-flowering plants so they could not self-pollinate. Then he took the pollen from the purple-flowering plants and pollinated the white-flowering plants. He was amazed when all of the resulting young had purple flowers!

What had happened to the white flowers? Somehow the white trait had disappeared in the first generation. The first generation refers to all the young born to a particular set of parents. Mendel was curious, so he took two of the first-generation purple plants and bred them with each other. Imagine his surprise when the white flower reappeared in the next generation, called the second generation. Some of the plants from the second generation had purple flowers. Others had white flowers.

Mendel realized that the white trait had not really disappeared. It was still there in the first generation, but it was hidden. The purple first generation was still somehow carrying the white trait, even though Mendel could not see it. He reasoned that the young received two units of information,

POLLINATION

SELF POLLINATION

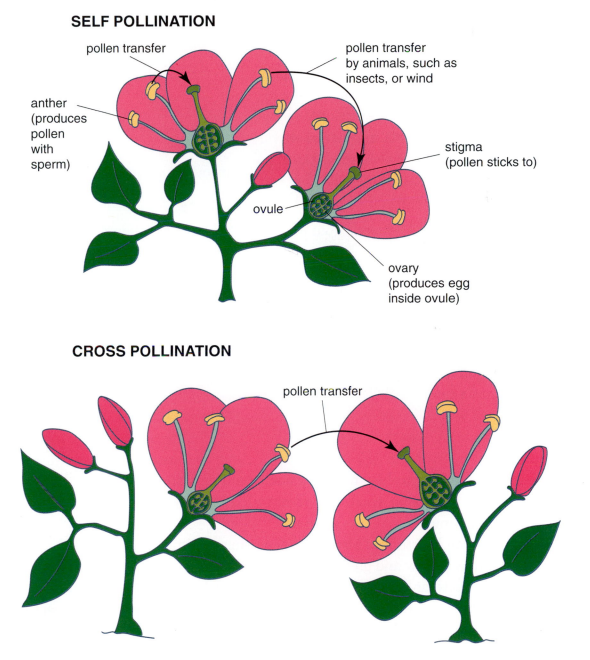

pollen transfer

pollen transfer by animals, such as insects, or wind

anther (produces pollen with sperm)

stigma (pollen sticks to)

ovule

ovary (produces egg inside ovule)

CROSS POLLINATION

pollen transfer

In self-pollination, the sperm from the pollen of one flower fertilizes an egg on the same flower or an egg in another flower on the same plant. In cross-pollination, the sperm from the pollen on one flower fertilizes an egg in the flower of a different plant.

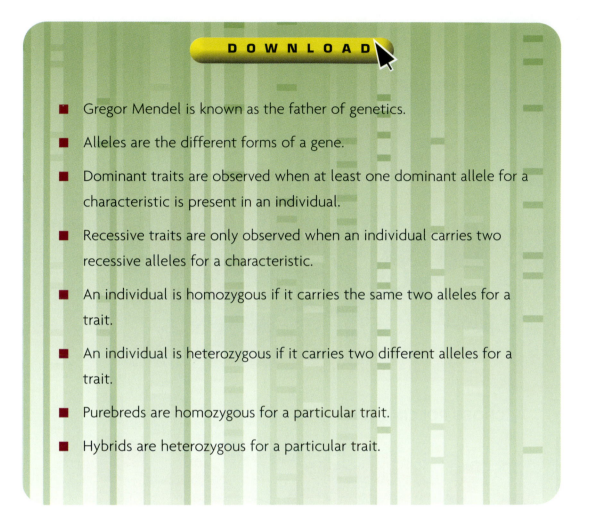

D O W N L O A D

- Gregor Mendel is known as the father of genetics.

- Alleles are the different forms of a gene.

- Dominant traits are observed when at least one dominant allele for a characteristic is present in an individual.

- Recessive traits are only observed when an individual carries two recessive alleles for a characteristic.

- An individual is homozygous if it carries the same two alleles for a trait.

- An individual is heterozygous if it carries two different alleles for a trait.

- Purebreds are homozygous for a particular trait.

- Hybrids are heterozygous for a particular trait.

one unit from the purple parent and one from the white parent. The characteristics of the young, then, were controlled by these pairs of units, which we now call genes.

Continuing his studies, Mendel chose other pea traits that had two forms, such as yellow and green seeds, smooth and wrinkled seeds, smooth and bumpy pods, and tall and dwarf plants. One at a time, he crossed two purebred forms and the same thing happened. One trait always disappeared in the first generation, only to return in the second.

Mendel explained this by proposing that, whenever a single characteristic has two forms, one form is always **dominant** over the other. The form that was not dominant, he called **recessive** (*ree-SEHS-ihv*). The recessive trait "recedes" or fades into the background. For peas, Mendel found that purple flowers were dominant over white flowers, yellow seeds were dominant over green seeds, smooth seeds were dominant over wrinkled seeds, smooth pods were dominant over bumpy pods, and tall plants were dominant over dwarf plants. Later, scientists would call the two forms of a gene, the dominant and the recessive, **alleles** (*uh-LEELZ*). All genes are in fact formed by a pair of alleles.

THOSE BOSSY ALLELES

Dominant alleles can be thought of as being the big bosses while recessive alleles are shy, quiet workers. If an individual carries two dominant alleles, one from each parent, the dominant trait will be evident. If the two alleles were talking to each other, it would sound like this:

The first dominant allele, screaming loudly, would say, "Hey, I'm the boss, and we are going to be dominant."

The second dominant allele, also screaming, would say, "Yeah, well, I'm just as bossy as you are. We ARE going to be dominant."

As a result, the individual would show the dominant trait. Of course, genes do not really scream, but the chemical proteins that the dominant alleles make inside the individual's cells would be strong.

On the other hand, if an individual carried a dominant allele from one parent and a recessive allele from the other parent, the conversation would sound quite different:

The dominant allele, screaming loudly, would say, "Hey, I'm the boss, and we are going to be dominant."

The recessive allele, whispering quietly, would say, "Please, sir, if you don't mind, could we be recessive?"

The dominant allele would scream back, "Be quiet, you little pipsqueak, we are going to be dominant."

The recessive allele, responding meekly, would say, "OK, I'll be quiet."

As a result, the individual would show the dominant trait. The recessive trait would be hidden because the protein it makes would be too weak to chemically overpower the protein made by the dominant allele. The dominant allele shuts out the action of the recessive allele. This is what happened to the first generation in Mendel's crosses. He could see only the dominant trait for purple flowers.

Finally, if an individual carried two recessive alleles, one recessive from each parent, the conversation would sound like this:

The first allele, whispering politely, would say, "Excuse me, could we be recessive?"

The second allele, also whispering, would say, "I wouldn't dare argue with you."

As a result, the individual would show the recessive trait. There is no dominant allele around to overcome and hide it. The only way a recessive trait can be shown is if both alleles are recessive.

When an individual carries the same two alleles for a trait, the individual is called **homozygous** (hoh-moh-ZY-gus) for that specific trait. Homozygous is from the Greek word *homos*, which means "the same." Literally, it means the zygote received the same alleles. If an individual has two dominant alleles, the individual is homozygous dominant for that trait. It will show the dominant trait.

If an individual has two recessives, it is homozygous recessive for that trait. It will show the recessive trait. However, if it has one dominant allele and one recessive allele, it is called **heterozygous** (het-ur-oh-ZY-gus) from the Greek *heteros*, meaning "other" or "different." The individual will show only the dominant trait because the recessive trait recedes or is hidden by the dominant trait.

Whether homozygous or heterozygous, the actual trait or characteristic shown by an individual is called its **phenotype** (FEE-noh-typ), from the Greek *phain* for "appear" or "show." Brown eyes, freckles, or curly hair are all phenotypes. Keep in mind, however, that not all phenotypes can be seen. For example, sensitive hearing and flexible joints would also be phenotypes.

The genes (or pairs of alleles) that an individual carries on its chromosomes are known as its **genotype** (JEE-noh-type). The genotype determines the phenotype. The genes make the proteins that determine which characteristics will show.

Scientists at the Human Genome Project in the United States have now identified most of the 20 to 25,000 genes found in humans. To map an

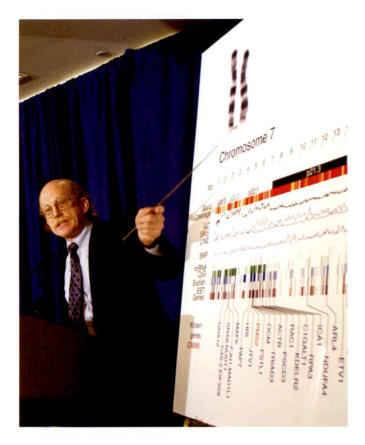

A scientist from the Human Genome Project explains the sequence of genes on human chromosome number 7. All of the human chromosomes have now been sequenced by scientists working on the project.

individual's complete genotype, it would be necessary to identify the specific alleles carried for each gene. Keeping track of so many genes is a challenge, so scientists have devised a system of abbreviations to organize them.

In many cases, the first letter of the recessive trait is used. For example, a lowercase *d* (or "little d") stands for dwarf pea plants, which is a lot easier to say than "the recessive allele for dwarf pea plants." The dominant allele uses the same letter, but in uppercase. Tall pea plants are dominant, so an uppercase D (or "big D") is used.

To write the genotype for an individual, the two alleles inherited from the parents must be known. In the case of dwarf pea plants, that would have to be *dd* (little d, little d), because the only way the recessive can show up is if it is homozygous. The genotype of a tall pea plant, however, could be either *DD* (big D, big D) or *Dd* (big D, little d). Both phenotypes would be tall because the dwarf allele would be hidden in the heterozygous individual. Notice that when the two alleles are written for the heterozygous, the dominant allele is written first, as in *Dd*.

Scientists eventually identified the genotypes of Mendel's peas. His purebred white-flowering plants were homozygous recessive, or *ww*. His purebred purple-flowering plants were homozygous dominant, or *WW*.

HYBRIDS

single hybrid trait for color (purple is dominant)

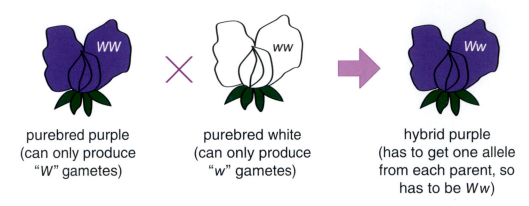

purebred purple
(can only produce
"*W*" gametes)

purebred white
(can only produce
"*w*" gametes)

hybrid purple
(has to get one allele
from each parent, so
has to be *Ww*)

Hybrids are organisms that have two different alleles for a particular gene. More than one gene also can be affected.

When he crossed the two purebreds, he created **hybrids** with the genotype *Ww*. Hybrids are produced by crossing two parents with different alleles for a trait. In this case, the hybrids got a *W* from one parent, and a *w* from the other parent. When hybrids are crossed, they no longer breed true or pass on the same alleles to every one of their offspring, which is why Mendel got both purple and white flowers in the second generation.

THE PUNNETT SQUARE

In the early 1900s, an English scientist named Reginald Punnett studied alleles in a number of organisms, including sweet peas. To keep track of his crosses, Punnett created a tool that is known as the **Punnett square.** Scientists use Punnett squares to visualize all of the possible combinations of alleles that can result from crossing any two parents.

To make a Punnett square, draw a large box. Divide the box into four equal squares. The male's alleles are written above the top of the box, one allele above the left column and the other above the right column. You can think of each allele as being inside one sperm. The young have as much

HOW TO DRAW A PUNNETT SQUARE

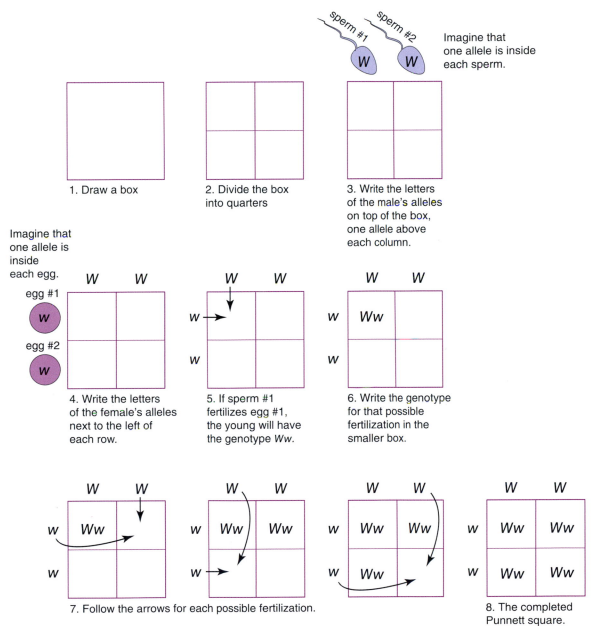

Imagine that one allele is inside each sperm.

1. Draw a box

2. Divide the box into quarters

3. Write the letters of the male's alleles on top of the box, one allele above each column.

Imagine that one allele is inside each egg.

4. Write the letters of the female's alleles next to the left of each row.

5. If sperm #1 fertilizes egg #1, the young will have the genotype Ww.

6. Write the genotype for that possible fertilization in the smaller box.

7. Follow the arrows for each possible fertilization.

8. The completed Punnett square.

A Punnett square is a tool used to visualize all of the possible combinations of alleles that offspring can inherit from any two parents.

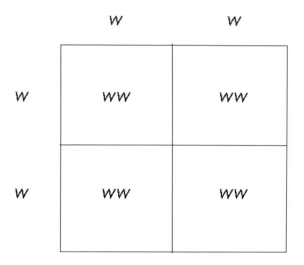

Genotype probability = 4/4 or 100% *WW*   Phenotype probability = 4/4 or 100% purple

chance of inheriting one allele as the other. The female's alleles are written to the left of the box, one allele to the left of the first row and the other to the left of the bottom row. You can think of each allele as being inside of one egg. Again, the young have as much chance of inheriting one allele as the other.

The four squares inside the box represent the possible allele combinations that can be created in the young. Suppose the sperm above the first

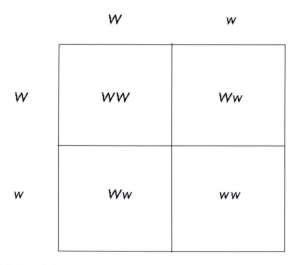

Genotype probabilities = 1/4 or 25% *WW*, 1/2 or 50% *Ww*, 1/4 or 25% *ww*
Phenotype probabilities = 3/4 or 75% purple, 1/4 or 25% white

column fertilizes the egg next to the first row. Put the two alleles together and write them in the square at the upper left. This would be one possible genotype that could be created when the parents reproduce.

TOOL BAR

	WG	Wg	wG	wg
WG	WWGG Purple, yellow	WWGg purple, yellow	WwGG purple, yellow	WwGg purple, yellow
Wg	WWGg Purple, yellow	WWgg purple, green	WwGg purple, yellow	Wwgg purple, green
wG	WwGG Purple, yellow	WwGg purple, yellow	wwGG white, yellow	wwGg white, yellow
wg	WwGg Purple, yellow	Wwgg purple, green	wwGg white, yellow	wwgg white, green

A dihybrid cross for flower color and pea color (*WwGg* crossed with *WwGg*, where *W* = purple flower, *w* = white flower, *G* = yellow pea, *g* = green pea). After performing monohybrid crosses, Mendel continued his work with dihybrid crosses. Dihybrid crosses pair individuals that are heterozygous for two different traits. Each parent can pass on only one of each allele at a time. As a result, 9 out of 16 should be dominant for both traits (purple, yellow), 3 out of 16 should be dominant for the first trait and recessive for the other (purple, green), 3 out of 16 should be recessive for the first trait and dominant for the other (white, yellow), and one 1 of 16 should be recessive for both traits (white, green). In other words, a 9:3:3:1 ratio. Mendel's actual results from his dihybrid crosses were very close to these predicted probabilities.

Suppose the sperm above the second column fertilizes the egg next to the first row. Write the two alleles in the square in the upper right. Continue in all four boxes, combining the male allele above each box with the female allele to the left of each box. The Punnett square will then show all of the possible combinations in the young. If a genotype is not in the Punnett square for that cross, then those parents cannot produce it.

For example, a Punnett square shows that if two homozygous purple-flowered pea plants (*WW*) are crossed, the only possible young that can be created are homozygous purple (*WW*) because *W* is the only allele that can be passed on in the parents' gametes:

However, if two heterozygous purple-flowered pea plants (*Ww*) are crossed, they could be either purple or white depending on which sperm fertilizes which egg.

The latter would be a monohybrid cross, meaning a cross between indi-viduals that are heterozygous for one trait. *Mono-* means "single." Out of

The gray wolf inherited its traits in the wild by natural selection. Those individuals with genes that made them better hunters were more likely to survive and pass on their genes.

Domestic dogs inherited their traits by artificial selection. Humans chose which genes would be passed on by selecting parents with the traits they wanted, and then allowing only those dogs to breed.

the four possibilities, three could be purple (*WW, Ww, and Ww*) and one could be white (*ww*). Using that information, you can then determine the probability for getting various genotypes from particular parents.

Probability is the mathematical possibility that something will occur. In the second example, an individual would have a 75 percent probability (three out of four) of getting purple flowers in the young and only a 25 percent chance of getting white (one out of four). If the desired result were lots of white flowers, these parents would not be used.

Punnett squares are easier to use if you look at only one gene at a time so that there are only four possible combinations in the young. To examine two different genes at the same time (a total of four alleles) increases the number of squares, and therefore the number of possible combinations, to 16. Three genes (6 alleles) require 64 squares!

NATURAL OR NOT

Normally, nature selects the alleles that allow a species to adapt to its environment. If a trait helps an individual survive, it will be passed on to the next generation. A trait that puts an individual at a disadvantage might keep it from finding a mate or lead to its death. The allele for that trait would die with the individual. This process is called **natural selection**.

Mendel chose the traits he wanted to pass on to the next generation of peas through **artificial selection**. For thousands of years, people have used artificial selection to breed plants and animals, favoring alleles that they wanted and eliminating alleles that they did not. Artificial selection was used to create purebred dogs. The allele for curly hair was selected to make a poodle and the allele for straight hair was selected to make a collie.

Breeders took dogs with the trait they wanted, say curly hair, and bred them with other dogs with the same trait. Although it was not necessary to know the genotype of the parents, it helped. But often, they would simply look at the young, and if a puppy had curly hair, they would keep it for breeding and those without curly hair would not be used for breeding.

The breeder would then continue to breed curly haired dogs until they got 100 percent curly-haired puppies every time. Essentially, they had bred

A tigon is a cross between a male tiger and a female lion. It is usually infertile and unable to reproduce.

out the heterozygous genotype. The same process would be used with many traits until all of the characteristics wanted for a breed had been "bred in." In the case of poodles, these would include curly hair, a long nose, hanging ears, and a particular size. In a way, creating purebreds is like cloning. Every individual has the same characteristics, so they are all susceptible to the same problems.

People have also created hybrids by crossing two different breeds of plants or animals in a process called **hybridization**. Instead of eliminating alleles, hybridization increases the number of different alleles in an organism. More heterozygous individuals are created, and fewer of the young look alike. Mutts are hybrids. Hybrids usually have fewer health problems than purebreds, creating a condition that scientists call "hybrid vigor."

Hybrids are often named by combining the names of the two parent breeds or species. The male parent determines the first part of the name, the female the last part. For example, a liger is a cross between a male lion and a female tiger, but a tigon is a cross between a male tiger and a female lion.

Although they do not follow this naming convention, mules are hybrids created from a cross between a male donkey and a female horse. Hinneys are a cross between a male horse and a female donkey. These hybrids, however, cannot produce young. They have an odd number of chromosomes, so meiosis cannot take place correctly, and for sexual reproduction by meiosis to occur, a cell must have an even number of chromosomes.

Horses have 64 chromosomes and donkeys have 62. Mules and hinneys have only 63. To calculate the chromosome number of a hybrid, the chromosome number of each parent is divided in two to get the haploid number, the number that would be in each of the gametes. These are then added together to get the diploid number of the hybrid.

Zeedonks are hybrids of zebras and donkeys. Zebras have 44 chromosomes, or a haploid number of 22. Donkeys have 62 chromosomes and a haploid number of 31. Can zeedonks reproduce? Zorses are hybrids of zebras and horses. The zebra haploid is 22. The horse haploid is 32. Can zorses reproduce?

A beefalo comes from a bison and a cow, a wolphin from a killer whale and a bottlenose dolphin, and a cama from a camel and a llama. Even dog breeders are getting in on the act. A cockapoo is a hybrid between a cocker spaniel and a poodle, and a labradoodle is a cross between a Labrador

A zorse is a cross between a male zebra and a female horse. It shows characteristics that were inherited from both parents.

retriever and a poodle! Breeders have also hybridized snakes, birds, bears, rhinoceroses, goats, and sheep.

Plants are even easier to hybridize than animals, and they often reproduce better than either parent plant. Almost every fruit and vegetable that can be purchased at a grocery store has been "improved" by hybridization. For example, wild species of apples tend to be small and sour. Hybrid apples are large and sweet. Many types of wildflowers have small, drab blossoms, while their hybrids are large and colorful.

By creating hybrids, scientists have made plants that are more resistant to cold, heat, insects, and disease. They have improved seeds, leaves, and roots. They have even created fruits without seeds, such as watermelon. If such a thing happened in nature, the species would become extinct!

Hybrids do occur naturally in the wild, especially along the edges of two different populations where related organisms meet. The resulting hybrids may be better adapted to the environment. New alleles might then spread into either population, changing the characteristics of the species. On the contrary, the hybrids may be less suited to the environment, and the resulting alleles may never spread beyond the edges.

Scientists are now taking artificial selection to a new level with the development of genetic engineering, where genes are taken from the cells of one organism and put into the cells of a totally different organism. Bacteria, mice, pigs, and cows have been engineered to carry human genes, creating hybrid cells. And to think it all began with a curious monk, Gregor Mendel. One wonders what he would think of it all.

The colors of many fruits depend upon the genes that control the amount of pigment produced by the cells. In eggplants (above), the more pigment, the more purple the color. If no pigment is produced, the eggplant appears white.

CHAPTER 4

The Forms of Dominance

Gregor Mendel was lucky when he chose the pea characteristics for his study. He happened to choose single genes that had only two allele forms, one of which was always dominant over the other. However, it soon became evident that not all genes behaved this way. Scientists now know there are many different forms of dominance.

WHICH GENE REIGNS SUPREME?

The form of dominance depends on how the alleles for a particular gene interact with one another to produce a phenotype. Homozygous individuals are not affected by the dominance relationship. **Heterozygotes** are affected because they carry two different alleles for a trait. Heterozygotes only occur in higher organisms that are diploid because a diploid organism's body cells have two copies of each chromosome. Dominance relationships do not occur in haploid organisms that reproduce asexually and do not have pairs of chromosomes.

The three basic forms of dominance are complete dominance, incomplete dominance, and codominance. Mendel's genes showed simple or

P O P - U P

Test yourself to see if you are dominant or recessive for each of the following traits. Test your family and your friends, too.

Dominant	Recessive
TOOTH GAP (space between the two top front teeth)	**NO TOOTH GAP** (top front teeth touching in the middle)
FREE EARLOBES (earlobes hang below point where ear attaches to side of head)	**ATTACHED EARLOBES** (earlobes attach directly to side of head and do not hang below that point)
WIDOW'S PEAK (hairline curves to a point in the center of the forehead)	**STRAIGHT HAIRLINE** (hairline is a straight line across the top of the forehead)
NOSE HOOKS DOWN (downward curve to end of nose)	**NOSE CURLS UP** (upturned curve at end of nose)
NONRED HAIR (any color of hair except red)	**RED HAIR**
BENT PINKIES (when placed side by side, top segments of pinky fingers bend away from each other at sharp angles)	**STRAIGHT PINKIES** (top segments of pinky fingers straight or barely bent away from each other)
STRAIGHT THUMB (last segment of thumb does not bend back at a 60-degree angle)	**HITCHHIKER'S THUMB** (last segment of thumb bends back at a 60-degree angle)
EYEBROWS SEPARATED (no hair in between the eyebrows above the nose)	**EYEBROWS NOT SEPARATED** (eyebrows connected in the middle by hair)

Tooth gap

No tooth gap

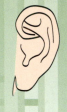

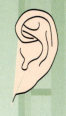

Free earlobes

Attached earlobes

Widow's peak

Straight hairline

Straight thumb

Hitchhiker's thumb

POP-UP

Dominant

COUNTERCLOCKWISE HAIR WHORL
(hair on crown of head grows in a counterclockwise direction)

CLUBBED THUMB
(end of thumb thickened or bulging out like a club or bulb)

COLOR VISION
(able to tell the difference between red and green)

OVAL FACE

DIMPLED CHIN
(dent or pit in middle of chin)

LEFT THUMB OVER RIGHT
(left thumb resting on right thumb when hands are folded in the most comfortable position)

LACTOSE TOLERANT
(can digest milk and other dairy products without discomfort)

Recessive

CLOCKWISE HAIR WHORL
(hair on crown of head grows in a clockwise direction)

THUMB NOT CLUBBED
(end of thumb does not bulge out)

RED-GREEN COLORBLINDNESS
(not able to tell the difference between red and green)

SQUARE FACE

NO DIMPLE IN CHIN
(no dent or pit in middle of chin)

RIGHT THUMB OVER LEFT
(right thumb resting on left when handsare comfortably folded)

LACTOSE INTOLERANT
(drinking or eating milk and other dairy products causes excessive gas, stomachache, or diarrhea)

complete dominance because one allele was always completely dominant over the other. Purple flowers were always dominant over white flowers. Tall plants were always dominant over dwarf plants. This form of dominance is often referred to as Mendelian inheritance.

Every person has a number of characteristics that were passed down through Mendelian inheritance. People who can roll their tongues into a "U" shape are dominant for that trait. If *n* symbolizes a non-tongue roller, and *N* symbolizes a tongue roller, tongue rollers could be either homozygous, *NN*, or heterozygous, *Nn*.

If one parent can roll his tongue (*NN* or *Nn*) and the other cannot (*nn*), then any offspring who are tongue rollers have to be heterozygous. One dominant allele had to come from the tongue-rolling parent (whether the parent was homozygous or heterozygous), because if a hidden recessive allele were paired with the non-roller parent's recessive, the offspring would not be able to roll her tongue. If both parents were able to roll their tongues, it would be difficult to tell the genotype of any offspring who may have inherited a hidden recessive allele from one of those parents (it would not be known whether the parents were homozygous dominant or heterozygous).

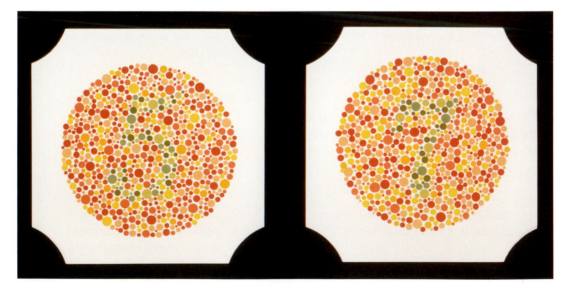

Color plates to test for color vision. If you cannot see the numbers formed by the green dots in the middle of the circle of red dots, you may have red-green color blindness. In other words, you cannot tell the difference between the color red and the color green. Both would look the same brownish color.

On the other hand, in the case of a non-tongue roller (*nn*) with two parents who can roll their tongues, both parents have to be heterozygous (*Nn*). One hidden allele must come from each parent. Finally, if the child is unable to roll his tongue and neither of the parents can roll their tongues, then it is certain that all three are homozygous recessive.

There is even a single gene with two alleles that determines how many fingers a person has. Oddly enough, having six fingers is the dominant allele. Five fingers is recessive. This means that most humans are homozygous recessive. This is an example of a dominant trait that has been eliminated by natural selection from most of the human population. Having five fingers must be a better adaptation.

BLEND IT

Incomplete or partial dominance occurs when a heterozygous individual shows a totally new trait that is not seen in either parent. The actions of the two alleles blend to create a new intermediate trait. Many flowers show incomplete dominance. For example, carnations and snapdragons have an allele for red flowers and an allele for white flowers. Because neither allele is recessive, scientists do not use lowercase letters to symbolize them. Instead they use R^1 for red and R^2 for white. When a purebred red flower, R^1R^1, is crossed with a purebred white flower, R^2R^2, all of the young are pink, R^1R^2!

Geranium flowers are controlled by incomplete or partial dominance. When a red gene from one parent is combined with a white gene from the other parent, the resulting plant has pink flowers.

Two sisters inherited different types of hair, one curly (two curly gene alleles) and one straight (two straight alleles). If another sister inherited one curly allele and one straight allele, her hair would be wavy because incomplete or partial dominance controls this gene.

Many fruit colors are also ruled by incomplete dominance. Eggplants are dark purple if they are homozygous dominant, but they are white if they are homozygous recessive. The recessive alleles cannot make the protein needed to produce purple **pigment**, so there is no pigment and the eggplant looks white. Heterozgyous eggplants are light violet because they only have one allele for purple and the other allele makes no pigment, so when the two are blended together the eggplant appears light violet.

People with curly hair are homozygous for one of the hair-type alleles, C^1C^1. Those with straight hair are homozygous for the second hair-type alleles, C^2C^2. This trait is governed by incomplete dominance, so a heterozygous individual carrying one curly allele (C^1) and one straight (C^2) would have a blend of the two, or wavy hair.

The size of a person's eyes, nose, and mouth is also controlled by incomplete dominance. Large eyes, a large nose, and a wide mouth are found in an individual who is homozygous for one of the alleles, and small eyes, a small nose, and a narrow mouth are homozygous for the other allele. The heterozygous traits would be medium, somewhere in between.

In codominance, neither allele is dominant over the other, but the two traits do not blend. Instead, both traits are expressed at the same time in a heterozygous individual. For example, cattle and horses have a gene that controls the color of their coat. An animal with two red alleles would have an all red coat and one with two white alleles would be white. But the two alleles together result in what is known as a roan coat, which includes both types of hairs. A roan coat has a base color, often red, that is lightened by white hairs. From a distance, the animals look rosy or pink, but on close examination the individual white hairs are visible. The same thing happens in erminette chickens. Their feathers are homozygous black, homozygous white, or heterozygous, in which case both black and white feathers are present.

In humans, the rare MN blood type is controlled by codominance. The two alleles, L^M and L^N, produce chemicals called markers on the red blood cells. The chemicals help the cells recognize which cells are part of the body and which are foreign cells that need to be attacked. Individuals who are $L^M L^M$ produce only M markers. Individuals who are $L^N L^N$ produce only N markers. Heterozygous individuals, $L^M L^N$, have both.

Chickens have two codominant gene alleles for feather color, one for black and one for white. When an individual inherits one of each allele, its feathers will have both black and white (speckled) feathers because neither color is dominant over the other.

A L E R T !

Receiving the wrong blood in a hospital emergency can kill you. If your blood does not match the donor, it will clump the donated blood and cause blood clots.

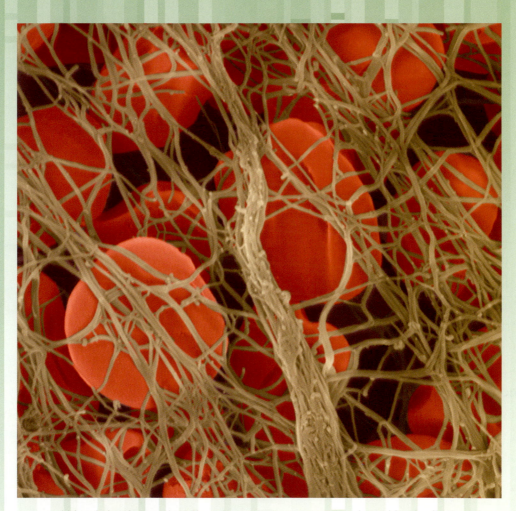

A normal blood clot forms when fibers form a net across a cut and trap blood cells. But when the wrong blood types are mixed during a transfusion, the red blood cells collect into clumps and block small blood vessels.

A FEW EXTRA ALLELES

The basic types of dominance deal with one gene and only two possible alleles. However, while an individual can inherit only two alleles at a time, one from each parent, many organisms have genes with more than the normal two allele forms. Such genes are said to have **multiple alleles**. For example, fur color in mice is determined by a single gene with several alleles, including black, brown, gray, and albino. Depending upon which two of these alleles an individual mouse receives, it will be a different color.

One form of blood type in humans is also an example of multiple alleles. A single gene determines ABO blood type, but three alleles are possible. The three alleles are I^A, I^B, or i. If a child receives an I^A from one parent and an I^A from the other parent, the child's genotype would be $I^A I^A$. With that genotype, the child's phenotype—which would be the blood type—would be Group A. The red blood cells would have A markers, which are one form of a special recognition chemical that acts against foreign cells.

If a child receives one I^B from each parent, the genotype would be $I^B I^B$, or Group B blood. The red blood cells would carry B markers, another form of the recognition chemical. If a child has one of each ($I^A I^B$) he would have Group AB blood. When these two alleles, I^A and I^B, are together, they are governed by codominance, and the red blood cells would have both A and B markers.

The O allele on the other hand, is recessive; it is symbolized by i. If an offspring receives one I^A and one i, the result would be $I^A i$, which is ruled by complete dominance. The individual would have Group A blood (the same as $I^A I^A$) because the A allele is dominant. These blood cells will only have A markers because the recessive allele, O, as in zero or none, does not make markers.

The genotype $I^B i$ results in the phenotype Group B blood. The B allele is also dominant over the O allele, and the blood cells would have only B markers. Finally, homozygous recessive, or ii, means Group O blood and no markers on the red blood cells.

It is important to know your blood type in case you ever lose blood and need a transfusion. Someone with group A blood can receive either A or O blood. The A markers on the blood cells will "recognize" the A markers on the other blood. The recognition is chemical. Because the chemicals are the same, there is no reaction. There are no markers on O blood cells, so there is nothing for the A markers to react to.

However, if a mistake led to a person with type A blood being given B blood, the A markers would react to the foreign blood, causing the B blood to clump together and form clots. If she were given AB blood, she would still be in trouble. The blood cells would not react to the A, but they would to the B.

People with group AB blood are pretty lucky, because they can receive any of the blood types. Their cells would not react to A, B, AB, or O blood. Individuals with group AB blood are known as universal recipients, which means they can receive any blood. People with group O blood, on the other hand, are known as universal donors. Blood banks are extremely grateful when people in the O group donate their blood, because it can be given to anyone who needs a transfusion. Because there are no markers in O blood, no other blood type reacts to it. Unfortunately for those in the O group, they can only receive O blood. Because they have no markers, they clump both A and B blood, as well as AB blood.

Clues for Figuring Out Dominance

Even if an individual's genes or alleles are unknown, it is fairly simple to determine which form of dominance they show. If a characteristic has only two different phenotypes, it must be controlled by complete dominance. For example, in studying a bug population, if only blue bugs and yellow bugs are present, then one of those traits has to be dominant over the other. The lack of a dominant trait would result in a third phenotype expressed in the heterozygote.

An assortment of blue bugs, yellow bugs, and green bugs would indicate that the trait is controlled by incomplete dominance. Green would be the intermediate heterozygous trait that was a blend of the other two. Blue bugs, yellow bugs, and blue-and-yellow bugs would indicate that the trait was controlled by codominance. Blue bugs, yellow bugs, blue-and-yellow bugs, and white bugs indicate multiple alleles, because one gene with two alleles can have only two or three phenotype possibilities.

Again using the bug example, if there were black, brown, red, orange, blue, yellow, green, and white bugs present, then the bug color trait is controlled by more than one gene. Such traits are called **polygenic**, which literally means "many genes." Human skin color and eye color are polygenic, as is

Two teenage girls display different hair and eye color. Physical characteristics, or phenotypes, such as hair, eye, and skin color are known as polygenic traits because they are controlled by multiple alleles. These traits vary greatly from person to person because many different genes influence the expression of these phenotypes.

hair color, which is why it is so varied, from light blond to black. At least four different genes (eight alleles) interact with one another to control hair color.

Various mixtures of pigment influence hair, skin, and eye color. A specific allele produces a specific pigment, such as black, brown, or yellow. Other alleles determine how much pigment is produced. Darker colors are the result of more pigment.

For example, people with dark brown eyes have several genes that produce a lot of brown pigment in their irises. People with green eyes have genes that produce more yellow pigment with less brown pigment. People with blue eyes have fewer genes that produce little yellow and little or no brown. The eyes appear to be a particular color because of the way light reflects off of the iris, just as the sky appears to be blue or red depending on how light reflects off air molecules.

But it takes more than genes to create the unique individual you are. Environment also influences who you become. The genes you inherit may determine your adult height, but your diet, exposure to chemicals, and the type of medical care you receive can also affect this measurement. If you inherit genes for taller-than-average height, but you do not get the right vitamins, minerals, and food while you are growing, you may end up shorter than your genetic potential.

Environment can also have a positive effect. If you inherited a gene that would make you more susceptible to a disease, but you ate right, exercised, and lived in a healthy environment, you might never get that disease. Your phenotype—the way you look and the traits you have—is determined by a combination of your genes and your environment.

A stem cell has the potential to become any kind of cell in the body.

CHAPTER 5

The Animal Body Plan

You are a unique individual with a distinctive body shape and face, but the human body plan is universal all the way down to organs, cells, and chromosomes. You have a stomach, muscles, and bones, your cells are animal cells and not plant cells, and you have 46 chromosomes. You are human.

PUT MY HEAD ON RIGHT

Genes play an important role in the formation of the human body. Everyone begins as a zygote—a single, unspecialized cell that scientists call a stem cell. The zygote reproduces, making more stem cells until it is a small clump of stem cells.

The stem cells transform into different kinds of cells, becoming specialized. A head forms at one end of the clump of cells and a tail forms at the other end. (Humans retain their tails, but they are very small.) Cells change into their adult form through **differentiation**.

Cells differentiate even though each cell in the body has exactly the same genes on the same chromosomes. So, if the DNA is all the same, how are different kinds of cells created? Specialization of genes is controlled by what are known as regulatory genes. *Hox* genes perform a specific type of regulatory function that has a particularly important role in the early stages of development. Hox genes determine where different body parts are located. Without them, your head might not be on top of your shoulders, your hands might be where your head should have been, and your feet might be sticking out of your back.

Hox genes are like light switches that turn on other genes. They work by producing proteins that bind to other genes and activate or suppress them. Those genes in turn may affect other genes. The process is comparable to setting up a row of dominoes. Once the first domino goes over, it knocks down the second one, which knocks over the third, and so on.

A Hox gene may start the process by determining where the head will go, which then activates a gene to form a brain in the head, then the eyes and ears on the outside of the head, and so on. Each part follows in line, one after the other. Hox genes are the same in most animals. Bugs, lions, and humans all have the same genes to tell their cells which end of the body the head should go on.

Human males have 22 matched pairs of autosomal chromosomes and one pair of unmatched sex chromosomes, called X and Y. The X is long and the Y is short. All of a female's chromosomes are matched because the sex chromosomes are the same, or XX.

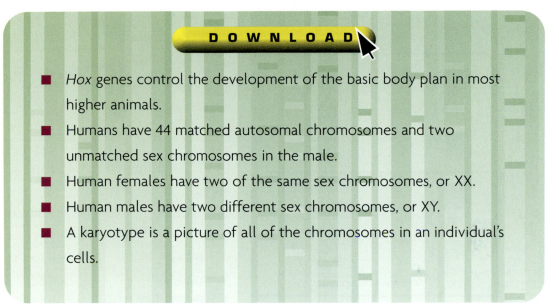

Genes are also responsible for determining whether a person is male or female. The 46 chromosomes can be separated into 23 pairs of homologous chromosomes. Twenty-two of those chromosomes match up perfectly. In other words, each pair has the same genes (but not necessarily the same alleles) in the same place along their lengths, like two peas in a pod. These matched sets are called **autosomal** chromosomes.

The other two chromosomes are called **sex chromosomes**. They are not matched in the male; one is long, and the other is short. The long sex chromosome is called the X chromosome. The short one is called the Y chromosome. The sex of the offspring depends on which of these is passed on from the parents.

IT'S A GIRL!

If a zygote receives two X chromosomes—one from each parent—it will be female with a genotype XX. If a zygote receives an X chromosome from the mother and a Y chromosome from the father, then it will be male (genotype is XY). Boys have fewer genes than girls, which can be easily remembered by associating the short chromosome (Y) with fewer genes.

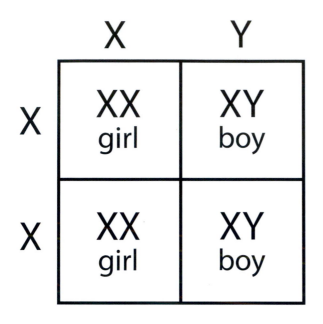

A Punnett square of the sex chromosomes that can be passed on by a male and female shows a fifty-fifty chance of producing either a boy or a girl.

That short little Y chromosome holds some pretty important genes that give males their male traits, such as the development of testes. The testes in turn produce the hormone **testosterone**, which influences the development of a deep voice, a hairy face, and a large Adam's apple, or larynx. Girls do not have a Y chromosome, so they develop ovaries and the female characteristics associated with them.

Notice that since females are XX and males are XY, it is the male that determines the sex of his children. Females can only contribute one X in their haploid eggs. But the male has a fifty-fifty chance of passing on either the X in one haploid sperm or the Y in the other. If an X sperm unites with the egg, the couple's offspring will be a girl. If the Y sperm fertilizes the egg, it will be a boy.

A baby's sex can be known well before it has grown into a human shape. Scientists can take a microscopic picture of a single cell in the early stages of mitosis and create a **karyotype**, which is a representation of the chromosomal characteristics of a cell.

To create a karyotype of a cell, the two longest chromosomes are lined up with their centromeres side by side. These become chromosome pair number one. The process is repeated with all the chromosome pairs in decreasing size order. Once the shortest autosomal pair (pair number 22) is lined up, the two remaining are the sex chromosomes. If both chromosomes in pair number 23 are long, the cell came from a female. If one is long and the other short, it came from a male.

ALL THOSE OTHER ANIMALS

The X and Y chromosomes determine sex not only in humans, but also in most other mammals. XX is female; XY is male. The genes on the Y chromosome determine the male characteristics. Some animals, however, such as fruit flies—those teeny black flies that sometimes buzz around your fruit bowl—have both an X and a Y chromosome, but the genes on the Y chromosome do not determine if a fly will be male.

Instead, fruit-fly **gender** has to do with how many X chromosomes a fly has compared to a different pair of chromosomes, symbolized by AA. If a fly is XX on the sex chromosomes and AA on the other chromosomes, it will be female. The number of Xs and As are the same. Sometimes in fruit flies,

SEX DETERMINATION IN FRUIT FLIES

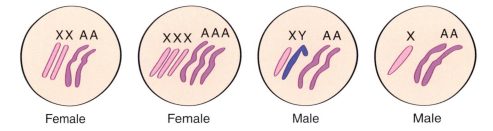

XX AA	XXX AAA	XY AA	X AA
Female	Female	Male	Male

A Punnett square of the sex chromosomes that can be passed on by a male and female shows a 50-50 chance of producing either a boy or a girl.

a mistake occurs during chromosome separation in meiosis, and a fruit fly ends up with an extra X chromosome and an extra A chromosome. Its genotype is XXX and AAA, but it will still be a female because the numbers are equal. When the number of X chromosomes equals the number of A chromosomes, a fruit fly is female.

However, if a fruit fly is XY and AA, it will be a male. There are fewer Xs compared to As. Even if a chromosome mistake occurred and a fly ended up without a Y chromosome (XO and AA), it would still be a male! O represents the absence of the second sex chromosome. There are still fewer Xs

P O P - U P

Because common fruit flies (their scientific name is *Drosophila melanogaster*) are small, easy to raise, and reproduce quickly, scientists have studied their genes more than those of any other animal.

Left: A normal two-winged fruit fly. *Right:* A gene mutation produces a four-winged fruit fly. Such mutations help scientists study and understand how genes work.

compared to As. When the number of X chromosomes does not equal the number of A chromosomes, a fruit fly is male.

The fruit fly does not need the genes on the Y chromosome to become a male. Instead, sex is determined by chemical interactions between the genes of the other chromosomes. The same thing happens in other insects, such as crickets, grasshoppers, and cockroaches.

The sex-determining system in birds is similar to humans, but in reverse. Z and W symbolize the two sex chromosomes. If an individual inherits ZW, it will become a female. Males are ZZ. No errors have ever been found in the sex chromosomes of birds, so scientists do not know which of the two genes is responsible for determining gender. In many organisms, the loss or gain of chromosomes ends in cell death, so those individuals would not survive to be studied.

Although not as common, many other sex-determining systems exist. Bees have a complex social order with a queen, worker bees, and drones. Only the queen is able to reproduce. Worker bees are also females, but they do not reproduce because of a chemical given off by the queen bee. The workers gather honey and take care of the queen and the hive. Male bees are called drones. Their only purpose is to fertilize the queen's eggs.

Female bees have 32 chromosomes, the diploid number for bees. Their sex is not determined by sex chromosomes but by a sex gene that has 16 possible alleles. If an individual inherits two sex alleles that are different (heterozygous), it will become a queen or a worker. The two alleles can be any of the 16 as long as they are not the same two.

Drones, however, have only sixteen chromosomes. They are haploid because they developed from eggs (laid by the queen) that were not fertilized. As a result, they carry only one sex allele. In the absence of a second sex allele, bees become drones. The sperm they produce is also haploid: clones of the drone. When the haploid sperm fertilize the haploid eggs, more females are produced, as long as the two sex alleles are different.

Occasionally, a queen mates with a drone to produce offspring with the same two sex alleles (homozygous). In that case, the young become diploid males. However, worker bees that care for the young quickly identify these abnormal individuals and eat them.

Only the queen bee *(center)* of a hive mates and passes on her genes. All other females become workers.

A few species of lizards, fish, and insects reproduce by **parthenogenesis**. Instead of producing haploid eggs, they simply clone their own diploid cells. No males exist in the population. All of the young are female. Because this reduces hybrid vigor, these populations are particularly susceptible to extinction.

Even stranger is a tiny tropical mite that also clones itself by parthenogenesis. It is almost exclusively female in the wild. It is also normally infected by a particular kind of bacteria. When scientists treated the mites with antibiotics to kill the bacteria, the mites laid eggs that hatched as males. Infection by the bacteria was affecting the sex of the young.

The environment can also influence gender in some animals. In many reptiles, it is determined by temperature. If eggs **incubate** at higher than normal temperatures, more males are produced. In at least one species of toad, males turn into females when there are few females available for reproduction, ensuring that the population does not become extinct.

In a few species of fish, called wrasses, the young are neither male nor female. The sex they become as they age depends on how many fish are around. If the population is small, competition for females is high, so fewer of them turn into males. If the population is large, more females are available for breeding, so more become males. In the tropical clownfish, the most dominant, or bossy, individual in a population becomes a female. The rest remain males.

In some cases, animals are two-in-one. For example, all earthworms have both male and female sex organs in their same body, so they can produce both sperm and eggs. They do not fertilize themselves, however. When they mate with another earthworm, the sperm from each individual passes to the eggs of the other. They both become fertilized at the same time!

Too many, or too few, chromosomes in a cell can cause disease, deformity, and death.

CHAPTER 6

Genes and Disease

For better or worse, your genes make you who you are. Your many different alleles give you variety and make you unique. Unfortunately, not all genes are perfect. Changes, or mutations, in genes can be good when they allow a species to better adapt to its environment. Other mutations create flaws in the way cells work. The effects range from mild to severe, resulting in illness or even in death.

THOSE PROBLEM GENES

Diseases caused by chromosome abnormalities or changes in genes are called genetic disorders. These disorders can be caused by cell exposure to a **mutagen**, which is an agent that increases the rate of mutation, such as radiation or a virus. If mutations occur in sex cells, they can be passed on to future generations.

Scientists who study how genes and gene mutations are inherited are called **geneticists**. Using a tool called a **pedigree**, they can trace the history of a gene in a particular family. The pedigree looks like a family tree. The traits,

Gene mutations can occur if you are exposed to harmful agents, such as chemicals, poisons, drugs, alcohol, pollution, cigarette smoke, x-rays, and ultraviolet (UV) light from the sun. Mutations can kill cells or cause disease, including cancer. If they occur in the body cells, they only affect the individual. But if they occur in sex cells they can be passed on to offspring.

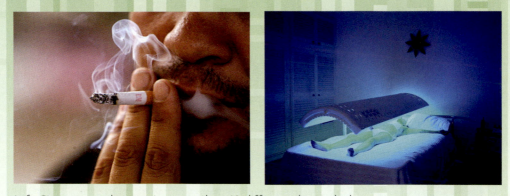

Left: Cigarette smoke contains more than 60 different chemicals that can cause gene mutations and lead to cancer. *Right:* Ultraviolet, or UV, light from sun lamps can cause gene mutations that are linked to skin cancer.

or phenotypes, seen in family members are indicated on the tree. From that information, geneticists make predictions about which genotypes the family members most likely have for the phenotypes. They also determine the chances that the gene in question will be passed on to future generations.

Pedigrees can be used to trace ordinary traits, such as dimples or freckles, but more often they are used to trace genetic disorders. They can indicate if a person might be a **carrier** for a disease. A carrier is a person who does not have a disease but is carrying the hidden recessive allele that causes it. If a carrier reproduces with another carrier, they could unknowingly pass the disease on to their child.

When constructing a pedigree, circles are used to represent females, and squares are used for males. A horizontal line connects the parents, who are

PEDIGREE

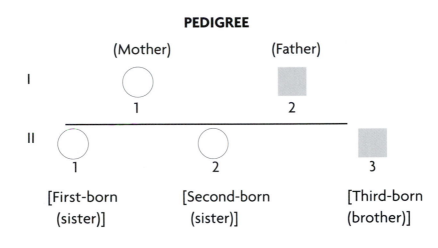

numbered. A vertical line drawn down from the parents' horizontal line indicates the children of those parents. If there is more than one child, siblings are placed from left to right and numbered according to who was born first. A horizontal line also connects siblings. Roman numerals to the left of the diagram indicate the generation. I indicates the first generation, II indicates the second generation, and so on.

If individuals have the trait that is being studied, their entire circle or square is shaded. If not, it is left blank. If an individual is a carrier, the left side of their circle is shaded. A diamond is used and left blank if it is not known whether a person carries or has the disease.

Most genetic diseases are caused by recessive alleles. In the example, assume the disorder is ruled by simple or complete dominance. The father has the disorder, so he is homozygous, carrying both recessive alleles. The mother does not have the disease.

However, the mother has to be a carrier because her son has the disease. She has to be heterozygous with one hidden allele. To show the disease, the son had to receive one recessive allele from the father and the hidden recessive from the mother. The two girls do not have the disease, so they have the mother's dominant allele. However, they are also carriers because they received a recessive allele from their father. That is all he has to pass on.

DOWNLOAD

■ Genetic errors that occur in gametes can be inherited.

■ Genetic errors that occur in somatic or body cells are not inherited.

■ A pedigree is a tool that can be used to trace genetic errors in families.

DOMINANT OR RECESSIVE?

Genetic disorders caused by a single gene mutation are much easier to study and trace. Most, however, are caused by a combination of genes and by factors in the environment. Mutations that cause disease may be found on autosomal chromosomes or on sex chromosomes, but wherever they are found they are influenced by the same dominance factors that affect other genes.

Human disorders that are caused by recessive alleles on autosomal chromosomes include cystic fibrosis, albinism, sickle-cell anemia, and Tay-Sachs disease. Cystic fibrosis is one of the most common genetic disorders in the United States. People who inherit two copies of a mutated allele produce thick, gooey mucus in their lungs, which clogs air pockets and makes it difficult for them to breathe.

Albinism is a recessive disorder that affects the gene that makes a pigment called **melanin**, a dark chemical that gives color to the skin, hair, and eyes. People who carry the mutations cannot make melanin. Several different forms exist, but in the worst cases, people with the disease have white hair and skin, pink eyes, and vision problems. Without melanin to protect their skin and eyes from burns and cancer, albinos must avoid the sun.

A single gene also causes the disorder sickle-cell anemia. Sickle-cell anemia causes a person's red blood cells (RBCs) to collapse into a spiked shape. These RBCs cannot carry oxygen to the cells, which they need to

A person with albinism *(right)* does not have the dominant gene alleles that give other people their skin color.

make energy. They also break easily and clog small blood vessels, causing severe pain. Without oxygen, the person gasps for breath.

Only people who carry two copies of the mutated allele are affected. Those who carry one copy as a hidden allele do not show the symptoms of the disease, although testing of their blood shows that half of their RBCs are sickled. Having just one copy of the nonsickling allele makes enough normal RBCs to keep these people healthy. They are carriers, however, and can pass the sickling allele on to their children.

Sickle-cell anemia occurs more often in people of African descent. In an odd twist, the allele that causes sickle-cell anemia also happens to kill the blood parasite that causes a disease called malaria. The mutation is both harmful and helpful at the same time!

Although less common, some disorders such as Huntington's disease, brachydactyly *(brayk-ee-DAHK-till-ee)*, and achondroplasia *(a-kahn-droh-PLAY-zhuh)* are controlled by a dominant allele. Unlike recessive traits, which can remain hidden in carriers, dominant traits do not skip genera-

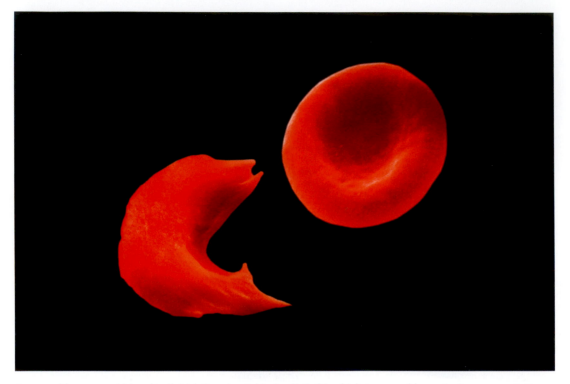

A normal human red blood cell *(right)* and a sickled cell *(left),* which is caused by a single gene mutation.

tions. A person can have just one allele and the disease will be expressed.

The allele for Huntington's disease makes an abnormal protein that destroys nerve cells. At first, the disease causes the person to make abrupt, jerky movements. Eventually, it causes brain damage and **dementia**, the decline of a person's intelligence and reasoning abilities.

Brachydactyly literally means "short fingers and toes." Many different forms of the mutation exist, but in all cases the fingers and toes do not grow at the same rate as the rest of the body. As a result, the digits are shorter by comparison.

Achondroplasia is commonly known as dwarfism. It is caused by a single allele that keeps bones from growing, resulting in a short stature and short arms and legs. People with achondroplasia, like others with genetic disorders, differ from everyone else by only one gene . . . one out of nearly 25,000.

A dwarf, a giant, and an average-sized human. Each person's height is controlled by different combinations of gene alleles.

SEX-LINKED DISORDERS

Most genetic disorders result from gene changes on the autosomal chromosomes, although a number are found on the sex chromosomes. These are called **sex-linked traits**. Autosomal diseases affect both males and females equally, but recessive sex-linked disorders affect males more often.

Remember, females have two long X chromosomes. For them to express a sex-linked disorder, they would have to inherit recessive alleles on both of their X chromosomes. Males, however, have only one X chromosome. Their Y chromosome is very short. Because of its length, the X chromosome has many more genes, so males do not have an allele on the Y chromosome for most of the genes on the X chromosome. If they inherit a single defective allele on their X chromosome, it will be expressed because they will not have a second dominant allele on the Y chromosome to mask it.

This makes it more likely that males will inherit a genetic disorder from their mother. The mother would be the carrier, even though she would not have the disorder. Males cannot get an X-linked disorder from their father, because the father contributed the Y chromosome that made them a male in the first place.

Alopecia (*ahl-uh-PEESH-ee-uh*), better known as male-pattern baldness, is a sex-linked trait. In order for a woman to show the trait, she would have to inherit the recessive allele from both her mother and her father. If she carried the trait as a hidden allele, however, she would have a fifty-fifty chance of passing it on to her children. If she passed it on to her son, he would be bald. If she passed it on to her daughter, the daughter would then

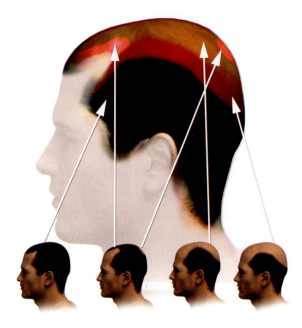

Alopecia or male-pattern baldness, shown progressing from left to right, is caused by a recessive allele that is passed on from mother to son on the X-chromosome.

be a carrier (assuming the father gave her a nonbald gene). The daughter could then pass the trait on to her son.

Colorblindness and hemophilia (*hee-moh-FEEL-ee-ah*) are also sex-linked recessive traits. Males are affected most often. The most common form of color-blindness makes it difficult for those affected to tell the difference between the colors red and green.

Hemophiliacs do not make the clotting factor needed to clot their blood. If they get cut, a scab will not form and they will continue to bleed. Injections of commercially made clotting factor can help to stop the bleeding.

An interesting sex-linked trait called hypertrichosis (*high-purr-trick-OH-sis*) causes excessive hair growth on the face and body. This syndrome may have been the origin of werewolf stories.

TOO MANY CHROMOSOMES

When gametes are being formed during meiosis, homologous chro-mosomes (anaphase I) and sister chromatids (anaphase II) are pulled apart and moved to opposite sides of the cell. Sometimes, however, chromosomes can get tangled and break during the pulling process or they can be pulled to the wrong side of the cell. In the latter case, one side would have too many chromosomes and the other side too few. When the gametes formed, they would carry the defects to any children that resulted from fertilization.

Most zygotes that receive too many or too few chromosomes die because they do not have the proper instructions to continue developing. But there are a few exceptions, such as trisomy 13, trisomy 18, and trisomy 21. Trisomy, meaning "three bodies," occurs when a cell ends up with three chromosomes at a place where there should only be a homologous pair. The number of the trisomy refers to the chromosome pair that would be matched up on a human karyotype.

Trisomy 13, also known as Patau syndrome, causes severe deformities of a child's face and internal organs. Often, they have extra fingers and toes. Children born with this syndrome have three copies of chromosome number thirteen, instead of the normal two. Fortunately, Patua syndrome is very rare. Unfortunately, children born with the disorder survive only a few months.

Actor Chris Burke *(front)* has Down Syndrome, which is caused by an extra 21st chromosome.

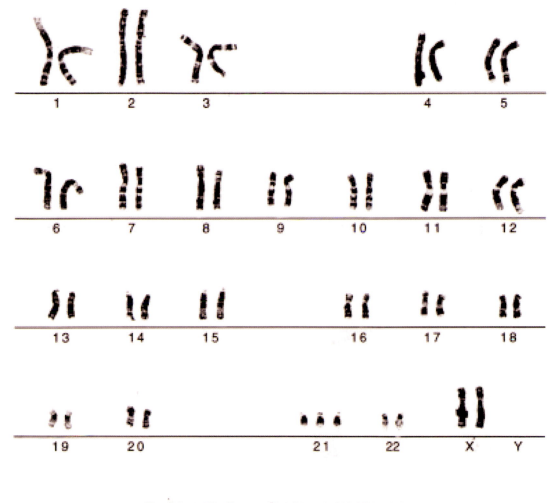

Female with Down Syndrome (47,XX,+21)

A person with Down syndrome has one extra chromosome at chromosome pair number 21.

Trisomy 18, or Edwards syndrome, also causes malformations, primarily of the head, neck, and hips. Again, these children do not survive. Most children born with trisomy 21, however, do survive. Trisomy 21 is also known as Down syndrome. Affected children have a characteristic fold in the corners of their eyes, stocky limbs and hands, mild to severe learning disabilities, and gentle demeanors.

GENETIC TESTING

An increase in information about genetic diseases has led more and more people to inquire about genetic testing. About 900 different genetic tests are now available. With a small sample of blood or skin, doctors can identify carriers, diagnose people with symptoms, or find defective genes in children before they are born and begin to show symptoms.

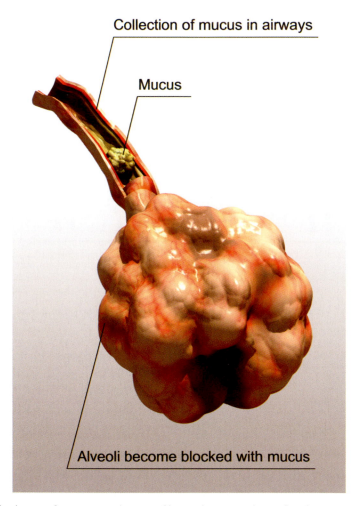

Collection of mucus in airways

Mucus

Alveoli become blocked with mucus

The lungs of patients with cystic fibrosis become clogged with mucus, making it difficult for them to breathe. One day, gene therapy may be used to cure the disease.

With this information in hand, people can seek treatments and make plans to manage their disease or the disease of their child. Some genetic tests even identify genes that increase a person's chance of getting a disease, such as heart disease, stroke, high cholesterol, diabetes, and certain cancers. They can then change their lifestyle, eat better, and exercise in order to decrease the likelihood that they will get the disease. You may be stuck with your genes, but that does not mean you cannot influence them.

Soon you may even be able to change your genetic makeup. Scientists are now experimenting with gene therapies that can replace defective genes with healthy genes. Healthy genes can be inserted into carriers such as bacteria or viruses that have also been genetically altered so that they cannot cause disease. They are then injected into a diseased organism. The healthy gene becomes a part of the organism's DNA and produces the proteins needed to cure the disease. Scientists are also working on a microscopic bead that can be coated with healthy genes and injected directly into diseased cells. This technology would eliminate the possibility of any side effects that could occur from using bacteria and viruses.

Researchers in the United States are experimenting with a gene therapy that uses a virus to carry normal genes into the lung cells of patients who suffer from cystic fibrosis. Working with the most common form of skin cancer, scientists in China have developed a gene therapy that injects healthy genes into the cancer cells to stop them from growing into tumors. It may not be long before genetic disorders are a thing of the past.

Glossary

adapted—having characteristics that allow an organism to survive under the conditions of its environment

alleles—the different forms of a gene

amoeba—a microscopic animal made of one cell, found in the ground and in water

anther—the part of a flower that holds the pollen

artificial selection—the process by which humans select desired traits in plants or animals, allowing only individuals with those traits to reproduce and pass on their genes to the next generation; also called selective breeding

asexual reproduction—type of reproduction in which offspring come from a single parent and inherit only the genes of that parent

autosomal—having matched sets of chromosomes

binary fission—type of asexual reproduction in which a bacterium replicates its single chromosome and then divides into two identical parts

carrier—an individual that is heterozygous for a recessive trait

cell cycle—the life cycle of a cell from the time a new cell starts growing until it divides into two cells

centrioles—small cylinders near the nucleus of a cell that form in animal cells during cell division and organize the spindle fibers

centromere—the region that holds two chromatids together after a chromosome is copied

chromatid—the name for each of the two parts of a copied chromosome during the time that they are attached together at the centromere; a pair are sometimes called sister chromatids

chromosome—the coiled structure of DNA and protein that forms in the cell nucleus during cell reproduction

condense—to pack more closely together

cross-pollination—the transfer of pollen from the flower of one plant to the female parts of a flower on another plant, either naturally by wind, water, or insects, or artificially

cytokinesis—the process in which the cytoplasm divides following mitosis

cytoplasm—the jelly-like fluid that surrounds a cell's organelles and gives the cell its shape

cytoskeleton—internal structures that support the cell and organize its structures

dementia—the condition of deteriorating mental ability

differentiated— having developed different characteristics

differentiation—the process by which cells change into different kinds of cells with unique functions

diploid—having two of each type of chromosome; having two sets of chromosomes, one set from the father and one set from the mother

DNA—the chemical that controls the activities of all living cells; deoxyribonucleic acid

dominant—in genetics, an allele whose trait is always shown in the individual that carries it

embryo—an animal in the earliest stage of development; in plants, called a sporophyte

excrete—to eliminate or remove wastes

fertilize—to cause an egg to begin to develop by uniting it with a sperm

gamete—an egg or sperm; a sex cell that carries half the number of chromosomes found in body cells

gametophyte—the stage in a plant's life cycle during which sperm and eggs are produced

gender—the sex of an individual; a male or a female

geneticist—a scientist who studies heredity and genetic variation in living things

genetics—the scientific study of heredity

genotype—the genetic makeup of an organism; can refer to one gene (one pair of alleles), many genes, or all of an individual's genes

haploid—a cell that contains only a single set of unpaired chromosomes; the chromosome number of a gamete

heterozygote—an individual with two different alleles for a gene; a heterozygous individual who produces unlike gametes and therefore does not breed true or pass on the same allele every time to its offspring

heterozygous—having two different alleles for a trait

homologous—the name for chromosomes that pair during meiosis;

homologous chromosomes are the same size and shape and have genes located in the same place (but not necessarily the same alleles on those genes)

homozygous—having two identical alleles for a trait

hybridization—the rearranging of genes by breeding individuals from different populations, races, or species

hybrids—organisms that have two different alleles, or are heterozygous, for a particular trait

incubate—to hatch eggs by keeping them warm

independent assortment—the independent movement of homologous chromosomes during separation in meiosis I

interphase—the stage in a cell's life when the cell grows and copies its DNA; the stage before cell division

karyotype—a picture of the chromosomes from a single cell, arranged by their length and centromere placement

meiosis—cell division that produces gametes or sex cells, each with half the chromosomes of the original cell; also called reduction division

melanin—a dark pigment that gives color to skin, hair, and eyes

metabolism—all of the chemical processes that occur inside of a cell

mitochondria (*singular*, mitochondrion)—cell organelles that break down food molecules to make energy

mitosis—cell division in which each new cell receives a copy of all the chromosomes from the original cell

multicellular—made of two or more cells

multiple alleles—three or more alleles of the same gene

mutagen—any agent that causes a change in the base sequence of a DNA molecule

natural selection—the process by which individuals that are better adapted to their environment are more likely to survive and pass on their genes to the next generation

organelles—structures inside of a cell that carry out specific jobs for the cell

parthenogenesis—the development of an egg into a new individual without fertilization

pedigree—a diagram showing the genetic traits of a family through several generations

phenotype—the observable traits of an individual that arise from the actions of the genes

pigments—special chemicals produced by cells that produce color

pollen—the tiny particles made by plants that contain the cells that will later become sperm

polygenic—a form of inheritance in which the expression of a phenotype depends upon the additive effect of two or more genes

probability—the likelihood that a particular event will occur

Punnett square—a chart that shows all of the possible combinations of alleles that can result from a genetic cross, and the probability of each one occurring

purebreds— individuals that have the same two alleles for a trait and always pass the same trait on to their offspring

recessive—in genetics, an allele that is masked in the presence of a dominant allele

recombination—the exchange of genes between homologous chromosomes by breakage and reunion

replicate—to make an exact copy of a DNA strand

ribosomes—cell organelles that produce proteins for cell growth and function

self-pollination—the transfer of pollen from one flower to the female parts of the same flower or another flower on the same plant

sex chromosomes—chromosomes that are involved in sex determination

sex-linked trait—a type of inheritance resulting from genes located on a sex chromosome

sexual reproduction—the production of offspring by meiosis, which produces male and female gametes, and by fertilization or the union of those gametes

species—a group of similar organisms that can mate with each other and produce fertile offspring

spindle fibers—fibers formed during cell division that pull chromatids apart and move them to opposite sides of the cell

sporophyte—the stage in a plant's life cycle during which spores are produced

stem cell—an unspecialized cell that gives rise to one or more specialized cells

strain—one of a group of related organisms that come from a common ancestor

testosterone—the hormone that is responsible for the maturation of male reproductive organs and other male characteristics

tissue—a group of similar cells that work together to perform a special job in the body

trait—a characteristic that an individual can pass on to its offspring through its genes

unicellular—made of a single cell

zygote—the first cell formed after the fertilization of an egg by a sperm

Search Engine

BOOKS

Alberts, Bruce, et al. *Molecular Biology of the Cell*. 3rd ed. New York: Garland, 1994.

King, William S., and Michael R. Cummings. *Concepts of Genetics*. 4th ed. Englewood Cliffs, NJ: Prentice Hall, 1994.

Marieb, Elaine N. *Human Anatomy and Physiology*. New York: Benjamin/Cummings, 1995.

Robinson, Richard. *Biology*. Farmington Hills, MI: Macmillan Reference USA, 2001.

Snedden, Robert. *Cell Division and Genetics*. Chicago: Heinemann Library, 2003.

WEB SITES

Science News
www.accessexcellence.org

American Scientist
www.americanscientist.org

United States Department of Agriculture
www.ars.usda.gov

Frog Genetics and Pollution
www.bbc.co.uk

DNA from the Beginning
www.dnaftb.org

Eurekalert!
www.eurekalert.org

Genetic Testing
www.familydoctor.org

Genetic Disorders
www.geneclinics.org

Human Genome Project
    www.genome.gov

Mite Genetics
    genomebiology.com

Hemophilia
    www.hemophilia.org

Genetic Testing
    www.mayoclinic.org

Cane Toad Sex Determination
    www.nrm.qld.gov.au

Human Genome Project/Oakridge National Lab
    www.ornl.gov

Index

Page numbers in italics refer to illustrations.

About the Author

Susan Schafer is a science teacher and the author of several nonfiction books for children. She has written about numerous animals, including horses, snakes, tigers, Komodo dragons, and Galapagos tortoises. Her book on the latter was named an Outstanding Science Trade Book for Children by the National Science Teachers Association and Children's Book Council. She has also written a fictional book about animal tails for very young children. Schafer has spent many years working in the field of biology and enjoys sharing her knowledge and appreciation of nature with others. She lives on a ranch in Santa Margarita, California, with her husband, horses, and dogs, and with the beauty of the oak-covered hills around her.

DATE DUE

AG 1 1 '11			
OC 0 6 '12			
JA 1 0 '13			